CHAMPIONSHIP DEFENSE

Proven Defensive Tactics That Win Games

Edited by Michael Podoll

Lessiter Publications, Inc. • Brookfield, WI

Publisher's Cataloging-in Publication
(Provided by Quality Books, Inc.)

Championship defense / edited by Michael Podoll, editor.—1st ed.

p. cm.
ISBN: 0-944079-36-9

1. Basketball—Defense. 2. Basketball—Coaching.
I. Podoll, Michael

GV889.C43 2001   796.323'2
                        QBI98-886

Cover photo by NCAA Photos
Cover and book design by Christopher Nielsen

International Standard Book Number: 0-944079-36-9

Copyright © 2001 By Lessiter Publications, Inc. All rights reserved. With the exception of quoting brief passages for the purpose of review, no part of this book may be reproduced in any form without the written consent of the publisher.

Published by Lessiter Publications, Inc.,
P.O. Box 624, Brookfield, WI 53008-0624.

For additional copies or information on other books or publications offered by Lessiter Publications, write to the above address.

Telephone: (800) 645-8455 (US Only) or (262) 782-4480.
Fax: (262) 782-1252. • E-Mail: info@lesspub.com.
Web site: www.lesspub.com

Manufactured In The United States of America

Foreword

DEFENSE IS ONE area of basketball where coaching can have a major impact. Even if your team isn't blessed with great shooters or high-flying athletes who can soar to the basket, they can still compete in every game by playing good, solid defense.

Through repeated practice, hard work, determination and by playing smart, your team can develop a defense that will be tough to beat. If you're coaching a group of talented athletes and they all buy into your defensive concepts — the sky's the limit!

Championship Defense: Proven Defensive Tactics That Win Games will arm you with some of the best defensive ideas from some of the brightest coaches in basketball today. Each chapter contains bits and pieces that you'll be able to add to your own defensive systems.

Old cliches like "defense wins championships" and "defense is the great equalizer" have their roots based in truth. We hope this book serves as the springboard for your team's defensive success.

— Coach Dick Luther
University of Wisconsin — Waukesha
Men's Basketball

"Defense will save you on the nights when your offense isn't working ..."

—Adolph Rupp

KEY TO DIAGRAMS

X   Defensive Player or player in line during drill

O   Offensive Player

●   Player with the ball

⌇▶   Dribble

⟶   Cut

--▶   Pass

⊢   Screen/Trap

"Defense is the foundation and heart of the game of basketball..."

—Jerry Tarkanian

Contents

CHAPTER 1 — THE DEFENSIVE FRAME OF MIND 7-27
Defensive Terminology *By Tex Winter* 7-8
7 "Little Things" For Big Defensive Results *By Pat Sullivan* 8-12
10 Ways To Sell Your Players On Defense *By Marc L. Comstock* 12-14
12 Rules For Sound Man-To-Man Defense *By Dennis Frisco* 15
Principles And Guidelines For Playing Outstanding Pressure Defense
By Andy Manning 16-17
Putting The Clamps Down On Defense *By Mike Madagan* 18-19
"22 Tough"—A Great Pressure Defense *By Christopher Kovatch* 19-23
Developing Championship Man-To-Man Defense *By Sam Santilli* 23-24
4 Keys To Playing Defense On The Ball *By Hal Wissel* 24-25
Employing The Press *By Robert Lehman* 26-27

GLOSSARY OF TERMS 28

CHAPTER 2 — FULL-COURT DEFENSE 29-47
Simple, Effective Full-Court Zone Press *By Peter Harris* 29-31
Run & Jump: Applying Defensive Pressure All Over The Court
By Don Horwood 32-35
"The Hawk"—A Swarming Press That Keeps Offenses At Bay
By Willie J. Banks 36-37
1-1-3, Full-Court Press *By Ed Webb* 38-42
How To Run The 1-2-1-1 Zone Press *By Ed Webb* 42-45
Pressure Defense As A System—The 2-2-1 Full-Court Press
By Buster Harvey 45-47

CHAPTER 3 — THREE-QUARTER COURT DEFENSE 49-64
Running The 2-1-2 Three-Quarter Court Press *By Rob Raque* 49-54
The Magic 11 Defense *By Don King* 55-58
The 22 Floater...A Three Quarter Court Press To Slow Down Good Teams
By Dick Luther 59-60
Using The 2-2-1 Dropback Zone Press/Trap *By Kevin Sivils* 60-64

CHAPTER 4 — HALF-COURT DEFENSE 65-84
Aggressive Half-Court Defense *By Steve Robinson* 65-69
Half-Court Man Defense *By Leonard Hamilton* 69-71
The "31" Zone Defense *By Thomas J. Moriarty* 71-74

CHAPTER 4 — HALF-COURT DEFENSE (Continued) 65-84
The 1-3-1 Half-Court Trap *By Mike Bartell* 74-78
2-1-2 Half-Court Trapping Defense *By John Ford* 79-83
2-2-1 Half-Court Press *By Buster Harvey* 83-84

CHAPTER 5 — SET DEFENSE 85-134
1-3-1 Passing Lane Defense *By Jack Thigpen* 85-87
The 3-2 Distorted Zone Defense *By Jack Fertig* 87-89
Playing Man-To-Man Pressure Defense *By Mark Comstock* 89-93
Try Man-To-Man Thumbs Down Defense *By Mark Porter* 93-96
Mixing Up Your 1-2-2 Zone *By Scott Barnett* 96-99
Man-To-Man Pressure Defense Revisited *By Mark Comstock* 99-102
Man-For-Man Multiple Defense *By Jim Baggot* 103-105
Man-To-Man Pressing Defense *By Pat Sullivan* 106-107
Using "Junk" Defenses To Negate Talent Differential
   By Kenny Edwards 107-109
Special Situation Defense: Tandem And Three *By Peter J. Grimes* 109-111
Unique Features Make The 1-2-2 Zone Adaptable To Any Opponent
   By Duane Estep 111-114
The "Gambler" 2-3 Trapping Defense *By Michael Smart* 114-116
Match-Up Defense Stymies Offenses *By Jason Wolfard* 116-122
Triangle And Two Defense *By Paul Basey* 122-124
23 Jump Defense *By Dick Luther* 124-125
1-3-1 Trapping Zone *By Wim Cluytens* 125-128
Using The "13" Zone Defense And Its Variations *By Mike Madagan* 129-131
The Rotating 1-3 And Chaser Defense *By Kenny Edwards* 131-134

CHAPTER 6 — SPECIALTIES 135-153
Many Ingredients For Success In Michigan's Post Double-Team
   By Jay Smith 135-139
Defending The Four Corners Delay Game *By Pat Sullivan* 140
End Of Game Defense When You're Losing *By Pat Sullivan* 141-142
Defending Under-The-Basket Inbound Plays *By Pat Sullivan* 143
Changing Defenses Scrambles An Offense *By Bill Graf* 144-147
Using Multiple Defenses Gives Your Team A Winning Edge
   By Thom Sigel 147-150
Defending The 3-Point Shot *By Roger Lyons* 150-153

Chapter 1

The Defensive Frame Of Mind

Defensive Terminology
By Tex Winter

A STRONG DEFENSE will be a stabilizing factor in the play of your team. It will keep you in games when your offense sputters and a good defense prevents disorganization. Defense wins!

Be prepared to play full-court, three-quarter court and half-court defense at any time. By doing so, your team will be capable of applying the types of pressure defense that complements the personnel you have on the floor.

Defense is an attitude which, if applied correctly, can be the most forceful weapon a team has.

The following are some terms that can help prepare you to develop a championship defense:

ARM BAR: Action of using forearm to body check offensive player.

"BALL" : Call to alert defenders of a loose or tipped ball.

CHASE: Getting on the assigned offensive player's hip and tailgate through picks.

CLOSE OUT: Controlled slide to cover offensive player.

DENY: Defensive play that prevents an offensive player from receiving the ball.

DOUBLE DOWN: Defensive double team on a post.

"HELP!": Yelling out a defensive SOS to your teammate.

INVERT: In stacks, defenders use principle of big players-in and small players-out.

"ISO": Call to alert team of an isolated offensive player.

ISOLATION: Term used to identify area outside of the 3-point line where the offensive player or players align themselves.

JUMP SWITCH: On switch, a move into the path of dribbler to influence either to baseline or stop advance of the ball.

ONE PLAYER REMOVED: Term used to signify sliding behind a screener.

OPEN UP: Defensive drop slide to an angle including ball and offensive player.

"PICK": Call to alert teammates to an oncoming screen.

POINT YOUR PISTOLS: Assuming a stance with one hand pointing toward the ball and the other toward the player being covered.

PURSUIT AND CUT-OFF: The defender runs, chases and slides to control the assigned player when beat or to activate a trap.

SEE THE BALL: Call to alert team or player to get ball vision.

SHOW AND RECOVER: Defensive action of simulating a switch on a pick and then retreating with offensive player.

SMOTHER: On the ball defensive overplay to force traps, jump balls, etc.

SQUARE UP: Defensive stance that includes bent knees, feet that are shoulder width apart, etc.

STRONG SIDE: Area on the ball side.

"SWITCH": Call alerting teammate on exchange of assigned players.

TIME DELAY: Defensive body check used to hold up offensive player.

WEAK SIDE: Area away from the ball.

7 "Little Things" For Big Defensive Results
By Pat Sullivan

AS JOHN WOODEN used to say, "If you emphasize the little things, the big things will take care of themselves."

Here are 7 "little things" that you may want to add to your program that will strengthen your defensive system.

1. AN AGGRESSIVE ATTITUDE

There are four times on defense when referees will allow your team to play aggressively. We have designed quick, 1-minute drills that will enhance this attitude of aggressiveness into your players during these four situations — loose balls, taking a charge, blocking out and guarding the ball handler when they pick up their dribble.

Loose Ball Drill: On the sideline, have a coach with a ball kneel between two lines of players. The first two players in each line get in the ready position and the coach rolls the ball down court. Each player yells "loose" and dives on the floor for the ball. The player who gets the ball passes back to the coach while still on the floor, thus avoiding the travel call. Your players should have the mind-set of diving on the floor after loose balls.

You have to practice this mind-set to have it happen in games.

Charge Drill: The same set up as above, but this time the coach rolls the ball to the left or the right. The player on the side where the ball is rolled gets it and the other player simulates coming from help side to ball side to take the charge.

Blocking Out Drill: Use the two free throw circles and the jump ball circle for this drill. Put the ball in the middle of the circle and have 6 players spaced in pairs around the circle, three on defense, three on offense. When the coach yells "now," the 3 defenders block out while the 3 offensive players try to get around the block out and pick up the ball. The coach counts to 3. Once the count hits 3, the defenders can secure the ball.

Ball Handler Pick Up Dribbler: Players partner up. Players with the ball take two steps right or left, stop, pick up the dribble and bring the ball over their head. Defenders belly up to them, cross their hands when the ball is raised, then mirror the path of the ball with one hand and keep the other in the high passing lane. As the defender mirrors the ball, they should yell "dead" three times.

2. TAKING CHARGES

If you are on the help side and coming to the ball side to take the charge, it is important to position yourself outside of the lane. Our film work indicates that if you take the charge in the lane, the call is generally a blocking foul, but if you get outside the lane, a charge is usually the call.

The players stance in taking the charge is of vital importance. Players can and do get hurt taking charges. Bend at the knees as opposed to standing straight up and down. This bend makes the opponent's knee contact a glancing blow instead of a full, forceful blow into your thigh. Second, with one hand, protect the groin area. Third, use your other arm in an "L" position in front of you with your forearm parallel to your body and at chest level. This is important because the rules allow defenders to protect themselves while taking a charge. This arm position enables the defender to take the brunt of the charge with the forearm, not the body. Fourth, upon contact, release your weight to your heels as you fall.

Players know that injuries occur when taking charges and they appreciate a teaching technique that gives them more protection from injury.

3. FAST BREAK DEFENSE

Use the terminology "fast break" defense as opposed to "transition" defense because it gets players back on defense with an offensive fast-break mentality.

We call the area between the two coaching boxes the middle third of the floor. A lot of victories are won in this area of the court. If you do not sprint through the middle third, you will not effectively protect your basket.

The Defensive Frame Of Mind

Always have the player closest to the ball immediately yell "ball" and pick up the ball handler. An opponent's outlet pass to start their fast break is usually somewhere around the middle third of the court. The recipient of the pass should be guarded immediately. The defender picking up this player should try to force a change of direction once prior to mid-court. This slows down the entire fast break and gives their teammates a chance to recover defensively.

The four other players should sprint through the middle-third area and when they get to midcourt, they should turn and call out which opponent they have responsibility for. It does not have to be the person that they always have responsibility for; they won't have time on a break to always find "their" person. Every opponent needs to be picked up by midcourt. This prevents 3-point shots off the primary break.

4. DISADVANTAGE DEFENSE

No matter how much you work on your fast-break defense, there will be times when your opponents will have a numbers advantage on a break. Preventing scores when you are numerically disadvantaged can be momentum breakers.

One-On-None: When an opponent has a breakaway layup, sprint down the middle of the floor. Because most players "show the ball" to the middle of the floor prior to their layup, go for the strip of the ball when they show it. Reach for the ball at the shooter's waist, as opposed to jumping into them and fouling. A real bonus occurs when you get the strip and the ball hits the shooter's leg. This not only prevents the score, but you'll gain a possession as the ball goes off your opponent's knee and rolls out of bounds.

Two-On-One: The one defender should set up above the 3-point line. From this position the defender will attack the ball handler with two objectives in mind:

✔ If the ball handler is out of control, have your player take the charge. Offensive players often pass off the dribble in 2-on-1 situations and are vulnerable to the charge.

✔ Attack the ball handler above the 3-point line. The one defender can actually get back to the layup shooter and block the shot or bother it. Pivot on the pass and swing the inside hand over the head of the shooter. By utilizing this technique, there is no foul because they kept space between the shooter and the defender's body.

Trailers must know exactly where to go. They should attack the player without the ball and try to steal or deflect the pass.

Three-On-Two: Instruct the two defenders to set up in tandem with the bigger defender above the 3-point line and the smaller defender at the basket. Many teams will shoot the jump shot on the 3-on-2 break and you want the quicker player going out to the shooter and the bigger player coming to the basket for the rebound.

Instruct players to attack the strong hand of the ball handler.

5. HELP-SIDE DEFENSE

Teach the basics for help side defense in terms of the triangle. There should be constant adjustment of the triangle as your opponent or the ball moves.

Stance: Players tend to get lazy on the help-side and when they get lazy, they gravitate to the high center. They literally play in a standing position and it limits their ability to prevent cuts and getting over to take a charge. Be sure the player is in an athletic stance, with knees bent, pointing to the ball and the opponent. In this medium center position, the defender can move with quickness to follow both ball and opponent.

One Step Off The Line Of The Ball: So many teams are now running motion offenses and because the primary screen in motion is often a down screen off the ball, be very concerned that help-side defenders get no more than one step to the basket side off the line of the ball.

While practicing your defense, have one coach watch players only on the help side. This coach can stop play to correct errors.

6. DENIAL DEFENSE

The only way to be truly successful in defending a proficient scorer is to give great effort before they can get the ball. Consistently denying a scorer the ball in their shooting range sends a clear message that if they are going to score tonight, it will be very hard work.

The defender should be in denial stance, but the primary point of emphasis should be the feet. Match the offensive player's feet. When you do this, you literally have your head in the passing lane and you make it difficult for the ball handler to pass to your assigned player. We call this "match-foot denial." When you play a team that widens the floor and emphasizes back-door cuts, go to a "split-foot" denial. In this stance, the back foot splits the opponent's feet.

7. SCREENER "EYES"

Guard down screens, perimeter screens away and block-to-block screens very differently. Players guarding the screener in each of these situations are really help-side defenders. They must understand that when the screens are set, they must be the "eyes" for a teammate who is being screened.

Teach those defenders to be head turners and keep constant vision on their opponent and the ball by quick turns of the head.

Abandon the head-turning technique when the player is being screened. When defenders are being screened, teach them to watch only two things, their assigned player and the screener. Don't worry about the ball. They

The Defensive Frame Of Mind

should literally turn their head away from the ball. They can do this because the person guarding the screener has become their "eyes." The person guarding the screener now has responsibility to watch their assigned player, the screener and the ball as they begin to quickly head turn because they are now the help-side defender.

10 Ways To Sell Your Players On Defense
By Marc L. Comstock

I'VE ALWAYS BELIEVED that you win championships with defense, and that the foundation of any quality program is based on defense. It doesn't matter what defense you play, so long as your players are properly prepared and motivated to play that defense. As a coach, you must understand the principles of your defense, how to drill the defense and, most importantly, how to sell the defense to your players.

The following ten ideas are extremely important in selling your defense every day throughout the season and during the off-season:

1. LOCKER ROOM SLOGANS

Every program should adopt several slogans that identify its defensive emphasis. Above our chalkboard is a sign that reads "DEFENSE WINS," and as players leave our locker room, they see another sign that says, "There is no homecourt advantage in rebounding and defense." Slogans such as these must be placed in strategic locations in the locker room for constant visibility. However, too many signs tend to dilute the message. Stick with two that are strategically placed.

2. PRACTICE GEAR

Every day, when our players put on their practice gear, they see "DEFENSE WINS" emblazoned on their shorts. We like to put it on the left leg of the shorts upside down, so when our players stretch or look down, the "DEFENSE WINS" slogan is readable. Again, a constant reminder, strategically placed.

We like to stay with the same slogan from season to season so we don't appear to be changing our emphasis. Also, changing slogans often may turn those slogans into mere gimmicks, rather than the rallying cries they're supposed to be.

3. DEFENSE FIRST

All of our practice sessions begin with our defensive warm-up drill, and the major portion of our first hour of practice is devoted to basic defensive drills that reinforce our individual and team defensive concepts. We believe that it takes "30 days to make or break a habit." This reinforces my belief in repetition beginning the first day of practice.

4. DEFENSE EFFICIENCY RATING (DER)

You must decide what defensive statistic is the most important in your evaluation of quality defensive play. The barometer of our defensive play is the defense efficiency rating, which is points allowed per possession. For example, 80 points allowed in 85 possessions equates to a DER of .94 or less than 1 point per possession.

We also place a tremendous emphasis on defensive points allowed, as we want to build a defensive mentality of not conceding any baskets during a game. Many coaches use scoring margin or defensive field goal percentage as a gauge of defensive effectiveness. Pick one or two areas you can emphasize and consistently refer to them in your evaluations and chalktalks.

5. GOALS

I am a firm believer in setting goals. We have defensive goals for the season and defensive goals for individual games. For example, we want to be nationally ranked in scoring defense for the season. We also want to be in the top third in our conference in all team defensive statistics. The game goals we strive for are as follows:

A. Grab 53 percent of all rebounds.
B. Allow 46 percent or less defensive field goal percentage.
C. Force a 22 percent turnover rate.
D. Hold opponents to less than 69 points.
E. Allow no player to score more than 19 points.
F. Shoot more free throws than our opponent.
G. Have a team DER under 1.0.
H. Win!

Goals give a strong barometer of how your defense is performing, and they allow you to focus on those areas in which your team needs to improve.

6. DEFENSIVE AWARDS

We give a Game Ball Award for every win during the season. To be considered for the award, a player must have turned in a solid defensive effort no matter how many points he scored or rebounds he grabbed. On rare occasions we give a "mad dog" defense award to someone who has an outstanding defensive game against a great player. This award is given sparingly, so it's very special.

We have also used the "star" program to recognize individual achievements in such defensive categories as deflections, rebounds, charges taken, blocked shots, help stops, etc., by sewing a star on the player's trunks, similar to the stickers you often see on football helmets.

7. DEFENSIVE BULLETIN BOARD

I like to put quotes about defense made by players and coaches around the country on our locker room bulletin board. When top college or pro coaches and players credit defense for wins, it gets our players' attention. Sometimes those people become your best assistant coaches. Players may be quicker to buy into defense when they read what others are saying.

8. PLAYING TIME

The real test of your commitment to defense is whether you reward people with playing time for quality defensive play and sit players for lack of defensive effort and efficiency. Anytime you ignore someone's defensive play for whatever reason, other players see through it. We believe you come from behind not with your offense, but with your defense. This dictates who plays, when we fall behind and need some defensive "stops."

9. DEFENSIVE CHALKTALKS

We always begin our preparations for an opponent by talking in a short meeting about how we'll defend them. Our last reminders in pregame talks will always include ways to have a quality DER. Our halftime talks begin with our DER and then move on to corrections and adjustments. At post-game talks, we always post our DER on the board. When it's below our game goal and we win, we make several short comments as to how we did it. When it's over our game goal and we lose, we talk briefly about our breakdowns, but always find one positive before we move on.

10. DEFENSE ALWAYS

I'm a fanatic about selling defense to our players, the media and other coaches. I want opposing coaches to respect our defense to the point where they made special adjustments when they play my team. I want every opponent to feel that no team on their schedule defends as well as we do, and that we are a special preparation for them.

Whenever I have an opportunity to speak at clinics, I want to talk about defense. When I work camps, I want the defensive station. When I write articles, I want to write about defensive ideas and concepts. I want our program to be recognized nationally for our defense. Most importantly, I want my players to feed off my intensity, energy and enthusiasm for defense.

I am fortunate to have had an opportunity to rebuild two college programs with a "defense wins" attitude. My teams have been consistently ranked in the top 15 in the country at the NCAA Division II level, and that's because we've taken a close look from every angle at how to sell defense. I hope one or more of those ideas helps your defense. Make your players believe they have an edge with defense by selling it.

12 Rules For Sound Man-To-Man Defense
By Dennis Frisco

MAN-TO-MAN DEFENSE is the essence of the game of basketball. The challenge of stopping your assigned player and taking pride in possessing good defensive skills are what competition is all about. Defense is 90 percent heart, determination, anticipation and hard work, and 10 percent skill. Good defense can rally a team, and good team defense is a true art when performed correctly.

Man-to-man defense is not easy to play and not for the weak-hearted. It is extremely vulnerable to a strong screening attack. Single, double and staggered screens test the mettle of a man-to-man defense. Some man-to-man defenses concentrate too much on the assigned players without the ball and lose the team aspects good defenses incorporate.

I am an advocate of aggressive man-to-man defense, a style that I believe tests a team's character. Good defensive teams work hard and together.

Following is a list of my "dirty dozen" rules for playing sound man-to-man defense:

1. Always concentrate defensive pressure in the area of the ball.
2. Lend vocal assistance to your teammate playing the ball.
3. Try to force your assigned player opposite to where they want to go.
4. Force the ball to the corner of the floor, where the sideline and baseline act as a defender.
5. Overplay the passing lane.
6. Retreat full speed into the paint and recover out of the line of the ball.
7. Retreat quickly and in straight lines.
8. Prevent ball reversal.
9. Prevent the offense from working in areas where they are comfortable. Take their first option away.
10. Have good weak-side vision and position. Think of where the next pass will go, then "react" to it.
11. Disrupt the rhythm and tempo of your opponent's offense.
12. Give up defensive ground grudgingly, and force the perimeter and post players away from their normal operating areas.

Coaches should not be afraid to challenge and test the character of their players. Man-to-man defense builds confidence, character and discipline. For this reason, an aggressive, hard-nosed, hard-working defensive team is postured to be successful every night.

Principles And Guidelines For Playing Outstanding Pressure Defense
By Andy Manning

I FIRMLY BELIEVE in the "defensive pressure" concept. In examining championship teams over the past few years, you quickly notice that those teams play outstanding pressure defense. It is my belief that by pressuring your opponent, you can cause turnovers that will lead to easy baskets for the offense.

In any defensive pressure system, three common factors are always present: Individual responsibility is always defined, constant pressure is always on the ball and help-side principles are incorporated within the system.

In an effective pressure defense, there are four items that are most important for players to be alert to. In order of importance, they are:

A. The ball. It must be stopped, first and foremost.

B. Their position on the floor and their stance regarding the ball and the basket.

C. Their assigned player.

D. The basket. They must protect the basket and not allow uncontested shots.

Why do we emphasize the ball first? Because doing so allows you to exert pressure on the basketball, plus it gives you the ability to obtain maximum help. This enables you to employ five-on-two, five-on-three and five-on-the-ball concepts, which give you the opportunity to incorporate individual responsibility and help-side principles in the overall defensive system.

Following are a dozen basic principles and guidelines for running a pressure defensive system:

1. Use short, concise verbal cues. They help players "coach" themselves once they realize what a technique looks and feels like. They also help players communicate with their teammates, which is an essential element in good defensive play. Finally, verbal cues force players to concentrate on the situation at hand.

2. Emphasize defense as the basic team philosophy and foundation, since that is the most consistent part of the game. It takes hard work and great technique to play good defense. I believe that anyone who wants to work hard and learn has the ability to play good defense.

3. Players must understand that defense starts with defensive transition, which means immediately after possession changes.

This can be created by a turnover of some sort, or, more importantly, defensive rebounding.

4. Put constant pressure on the basketball — when it is held, when it is dribbled, when it is passed and when it is shot. This kind of pressure minimizes the amount of free thinking time available to the offensive player.
5. Deny one pass away from the ball. Push the ball to the side and deny it from reversing.
6. Give help-side support. This allows you to give maximum help to the ball-side defenders.
7. Each defender must be responsible for everyone else's assigned player in the team defensive concept.
8. Use the "closest defender" concept. The closest defender to the ball takes the ball.
9. All techniques, concepts and principles must be learned through repetition and played with perfection.
10. Everyone must thoroughly understand what you are trying to accomplish with a pressure defense. This requires knowledge and understanding of the entire defensive system, plus a 100-percent effort mentally at all times.
11. Every player must play as hard as they can for as long as they can. Players must understand that there is no rest on the court; they can rest on the bench. They must give a 100-percent effort physically at all times.
12. All players must learn to defend. A player can't earn playing time without playing defense.

For your team to reach its potential and to be successful utilizing the defensive pressure system, your players must satisfy the following criteria:

✔ They must believe totally in the system and enjoy the challenge it takes to be successful playing pressure defense.

✔ They must play aggressively using the correct technique.

✔ They must learn the basic techniques, concepts and principles, which must be applied in every situation.

✔ They must communicate with teammates and with coaches. Communication is a key factor in defensive success.

"Winning is more related to good defense than good offense."

—Jack Ramsey

Putting The Clamps Down On Defense
By Mike Madagan

WHY PRESS?
✔ Pressing makes your superior conditioning a factor during the last 5 minutes of the game.
✔ It allows you to develop quality depth and play 9 or 10 players in each game.
✔ It disrupts the opposing offense, speeds up their tempo and forces them to take the majority of their shots from a free lance situation.
✔ Increases both game and practice intensity.
✔ Players, fans and media enjoy watching this style of play.

CHARACTERISTICS OF A GOOD PRESSING TEAM
1. Superior conditioning.
2. Quality depth.
3. The coaching staff's commitment to that style of play.
4. Quality of scouting.
5. Maximum intensity.

EFFECTIVE PRESSING TEAMS
✔ Put great pressure on the ball.
✔ Communicate.
✔ Sprint out of traps and recover.
✔ Limit two-on-one situations.
✔ Only trap uncontrolled dribblers.
✔ Use the sideline and baseline as extra defenders.
✔ Eliminate second shots by blocking out in transition.
✔ Understand that constant pressure wears down an opponent and that steals may not occur early.
✔ Force the other team to have non-ball handlers make decisions.
✔ Make conditioning become a factor in the game.
✔ Realize a quick shot is as good

15 IDEAS FOR DEFENSIVE GROWTH
HERE'S WHAT'S IMPORTANT to work on with your players to develop good defensive habits.
1. Stance on and off the ball.
2. Contesting every shot.
3. Pressure on the ball, hands tracing ball and hands up.
4. Getting the ball out of the middle of the floor.
5. Contesting all breaks.
6. Closing-out on all shooters.
7. Fighting for post position.
8. Help and recovery.
9. Defensive transition.
10. Blocking out.
11. Taking charges.
12. Rotating on baseline penetrations.
13. Doubling on all post passes.
14. Switching, fighting through screens.
15. Diving for loose balls.

as a turnover.

Playing on a 94 by 50 foot court is demanding. Anything short of maximum effort from your team will result in less than acceptable results. Thus it is important to design drills so that your team's press remains fresh and competitive.

KEY CONCEPTS FOR POST DEFENSE

➤ **Fighting Low Post "Duck-In":** On duck-in action, have your player step over the top leg and force the offensive player off desired area.

➤ **Getting Your Opponent Off The Block:** Teach your players to position themselves on the offensive player thigh-on-thigh, lock the leg in and push the opponent off. They should keep their hands high, so not to get called for fouls.

➤ **Block-To-Block Screens:** The player defending the screener follows the screener while having vision on the basketball. The player who is defending the opponent coming off the screen gets above the screen while pushing down on the screener.

➤ **Baseline Penetration:** It is essential that defenders meet the penetration outside the lane area and seal down on the block.

➤ **Doubling In The Low Post:** Your players should double from the inside with hands up high and put their body on the post player. If the pass is made from the wing to the baseline side of the post, you should double big-to-big off the weak side. You must then seal down inside the weak-side post player.

"22 Tough" — A Great Pressure Defense
By Christopher Kovatch

THERE IS AN old adage that "defense wins for your team." However, it's my view that "pressure defense wins for your team."

Starting from ground zero is no easy task in whatever you do in life. One year, our coaching staff inherited a team that was winless in 30 games the previous season. Installing and executing pressure man-to-man defense made rebuilding our team a little bit easier.

The athletes were there (although none very tall); they were quick, but also very fundamentally behind. The first thing we taught them was how to play a system of defense. This was a large task, as they had never heard of a defense having a concept or goals associated with it other than denying shots.

Day-by-day we installed the 22-Tough, our pressure man-to-man defense. The 22-Tough features several principles based upon logic and rely on speed.

OBJECTIVES

Our number one objective is to keep the ball out of the paint. Everyone knows that the highest percentage shots come from within the paint, so it's critical to keep your opponents out of the paint.

Any shot the offense takes should be a low-percentage one (low-percentage shots encompass shots from behind the backboard, shots from way downtown, off-balance shots or any shot outside the paint where your players have at least a hand in someone's face). Your defense should create as many turnovers as possible by inviting the long pass to an opponent that "appears" open.

CONCEPTS

You accomplish this in a number of ways. First, try to force the ball to one side of the floor and keep it there by denying the offense the ability to see the other side of the floor and by denying the short pass across the court. The ability to keep the ball on one side of the floor can't be emphasized enough.

Have your players push the ball to the baseline or sideline. Only three of the offense's five players can be effective with the ball at one time. With the sideline and baseline working on your behalf, you can have seven effective members of your defense working together.

All five defensive players must be attuned to the ball and the player's they are defending at all times. A key phrase is "see man-see ball." The players' primary focus is how the ball's location dictates how they should defend the assigned player.

FOR GUARDS

If a guard's assigned player has possession of the ball, they must force that player down into the baseline and as far out from the paint as possible. They also try to invite passes further into the baseline, yet away from the paint. Guards defending a player without the ball, but on the same side of the floor as the ball, must deny the pass to the top of the floor if their assigned player is above the ball and invite the pass to the baseline if positioned below the ball.

If the assigned opponent is on the opposite side of the ball or on the "help side," the defender must get position in the paint, between the ball and the assigned player. The defender must deny the flash by the assigned player, provide help to deny shots in the paint and invite a lob pass if the assigned player is roughly 20 feet or more away from the ball.

POST PLAYERS

Whether ball side or help side, post players must front their opponents all the time. They must constantly fight and reposition themselves to control the opposing post players. Their best line of defense lies in not allowing the opponents they're guarding to ever look open. If one offensive post player gets the ball, the help-side defensive post defender must rush in to deny the shot, get in position to take the charge or block the ball.

ALIGNMENT

Knowing that there are a fixed number of sets that an offense can line up in (1-2-2, 1-3-1, 1-4, etc.) you should essentially try to mimic them in your starting alignment. One of the biggest keys in your initial alignment is for every defensive player, except for X1 (the player guarding the ball when it crosses half court) to begin by having at least one foot in the paint. X1 must push the ball down to the corner of the court to take advantage of the boundary lines.

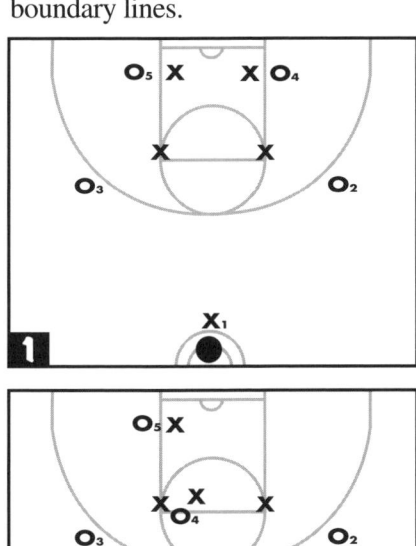

Diagram 1: Initial alignment against a 1-2-2 set.
Diagram 2: Alignment against a 1-3-1.

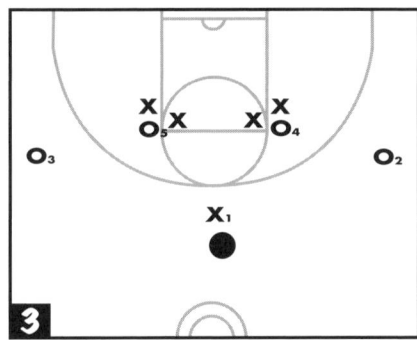

Diagram 3: Alignment against a 1-4 variation.

HELPING OUT

Although all of your defenders are trying to force the ball to do certain things, they can't forget the one concept that denies high-percentage shots and creates turnovers. All five defenders on the floor must be ready to provide help at any time. Whether it be an offensive player driving to the goal, a screen, a pick-and-roll or an entry pass to the post over a fronting defender, you should have at least one defender stepping in to prevent the high-percentage shot.

Have your players think of the defense as being a zone when the paint is challenged because they know that they must all defend it.

The key to providing proper help relies on the ability of the defensive players to over-rotate. Pure rotating is not enough; your defense needs to be consistently over-rotating.

In diagrams 4, 5 and 6, note the

pressure forced on the ball and the adjustments made by the five defensive players to force the ball out of the paint to the sideline and corner of the court.

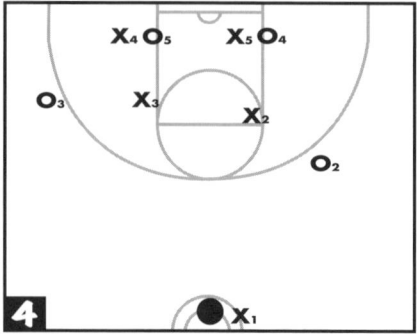

Diagram 4: Defender X1 applies pressure to the ball to "begin the push to the corner." X1 must play aggressive pressure defense and position their body in a manner that prevents penetration, but forces the push downward. X3 adjusts to the ball's location by stepping into position to prevent 1s drive and invites the ball handler to pass the ball to the 3 guard. Inviting this pass allows the ball to be pushed further into the corner.

X4 and X5 front the post players while X2 drops to a position where X2 can give back-side help and still watch the assigned player.

Diagram 5: The 3 guard now has the ball. X3 now takes the position that X1 had in diagram 4. X3 must continue the push to the corner. X4 and X5 continue to front the posts while X1 drops to a help position with X2.

X1 and X2 rely on the fact that X3 will not let the ball come back up the floor and cross the court. However, they position themselves "one pass" away from the ball and their assigned player.

X2 has one foot in the paint because X2's assigned player is away from the ball and not a threat. It will take 2 cutting towards the ball, a lob or a long skip pass to get the ball over. If 2 cuts, your defenders should deny it. If either of the passes are thrown, your players should realize that if they anticipate, they can get a steal.

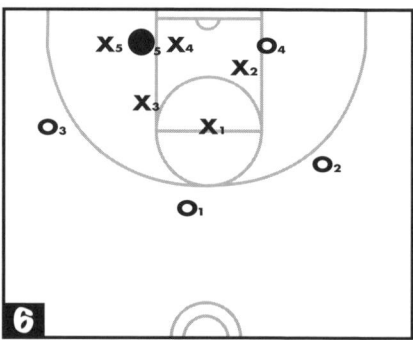

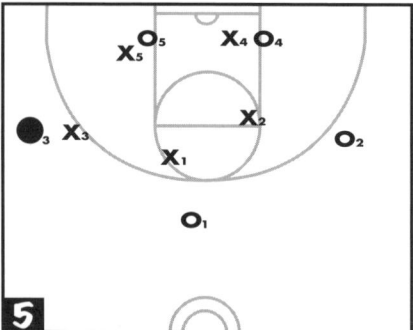

Diagram 6: 5 has gotten the ball over or around X5. This can often happen if your team is undersized, but the principles of pressure defenses are molded to this factor. Note how X4 has left the assigned player to take position underneath

5. X4 will attempt to take a charge and/or deny a shot. X2 has dropped to front 4 (never leave a post unfronted).

X3 and X1 have also dropped into position to prevent passes, which will lead to high-percentage baskets.

Developing Championship Man-To-Man Defense
By Sam Santilli

IF YOU CAN stop the other team from scoring, you can stay in a game and have a chance to win.

No matter how bad a game a player is having on offense, they should still be able to play smart team defense.

Players can be taught to play good man-to-man defense regardless of their size or speed. All they have to do is use the proper techniques.

The techniques of staying between their player and the basket if they are "on-the-ball," or being between the ball and their player if they are "off-the-ball," are essential to the success of team defense.

Once players understand the basic concept of seeing the ball and their player at all times, you can teach a variety of match-up zones with different traps.

Since the principles of help and recover, jump, deny and rotate are basically the same in man and zone defenses, choose a style that fits your team's strengths.

The chart below lists many of the important ingredients needed for playing championship quality man-to-man defense.

ABC's OF CHAMPIONSHIP DEFENSE

Always play aggressive and intense in practice and games.

Box out properly to limit opponents to one shot and out.

Closeout on the perimeter and contain the dribbler.

Deny all cutters and flashers in the lane.

Eliminate dribble penetration.

Force the ball to the sideline and force bad shots. Fight like heck to get through picks and screens.

Get back on defense quickly when in transition. Stop the ball and match up.

Help and recover if a teammate is beaten.

If the ball is ahead of you in transition, sprint to chase and back tip or fill the passing lane.

Jam the rebounder to slow down any fast breaks in transition.

The Defensive Frame Of Mind

Keep the ball out of the lane. Use some type of double- down strategy to help if the ball does get in there.

Locate the ball and your player at all times. Point to both as a constant reminder if you are "off-the-ball."

Move on the pass, not the catch.

No uncontested shots are allowed.

Out-hustle your opponent to all loose balls and rebounds.

Pressure the ball at all times and take pride in your defense.

Quick hands and feet are a must. Play on the balls of your feet, not your heels.

Read the passer's eyes and shoulders and anticipate the pass so you can deflect or steal it.

Stay low, shuffle and slide your feet when playing "on-the-ball."

Talk on defense. Call out cutters, screens, picks, skip passes and shots.

Use defensive fakes to force bad passes and shots.

Visualize yourself in a flat triangle between the ball and your player.

Weak-side defenders are responsible for back door cuts, cross-court passes and lobs into the post.

X marks the spot. Beat a player to the spot on defense and draw the charge, or at least stop the drive.

Yell "shot" every time the opponent shoots to warn teammates to get in position to box out and rebound.

Zero layup rule is in effect at all times.

4 Keys To Playing Defense On The Ball
By Hal Wissel

THE MOST VITAL aspect of playing great defense is pressuring the dribbler. Pressuring the opposition's point guard and best ball handler throughout the game prevents your opponent from focusing on running an effective offense.

Where on the court your players pick up the dribbler (full court, half court, top of the circle, etc.) will be determined by team strategy. When your players are guarding an opponent with the ball, the position they should maintain is between their opponent and the basket.

Tell your players they must strive to give ground grudgingly. Whenever possible, your players should force their opponent to pick up the dribble. Then they can apply more pressure against a shot or a pass, with both hands up.

The following four basic situations determine how your team's defensive strategy establishes the position your players should take.

1. TURNING THE DRIBBLER

The basic idea in turning the dribbler, or forcing the reverse dribble, is to dominate your opponent by applying maximum pressure on the ball. Players should establish defensive position a half-body ahead in the direction in which the dribbler wants to go.

This is called "chest on the ball." The objective is to prevent strong-side movement and force the dribbler into a reverse dribble. With good anticipation, your defender may even draw a charge.

If the dribbler tries a front change-of-direction, your player should be able to steal the ball with a quick flick upward of his or her near hand. On the dribbler's reverse dribble, your defender should quickly change direction and again move to the chest-on-the-ball position, at least a half-body ahead of the direction the dribbler wants to go. Your players should continue forcing the dribbler to reverse turn.

2. FORCING THE DRIBBLER SIDELINE

When forced to the sideline, the dribbler can pass in only one direction and the sideline can serve as a defensive aid. Have your players work for position a half-body to the inside of the court, with their inside (closer to the middle) foot forward and their outside foot back.

The dribbler must be forced to the sideline. Make sure your defender does not allow a reverse dribble back to the middle of the court. By dribbling to the middle, the dribbler has more options to pass to either side or to attempt a high-percentage shot.

3. FUNNELING DRIBBLER TO MIDDLE

By taking a defensive position a half-body to the outside of the court, your players can funnel the dribbler to the middle. This strategy will move the dribbler toward your player's defensive teammates off the ball. In turn, your players can use teaming tactics, including a switch, fake switch, trap or steal.

If your team has a shot blocker, you may benefit by funneling the dribbler in the direction of the shot blocker. The danger in funneling the dribbler to the middle is allowing the offensive player to move by the defender and into a chance to penetrate the lane for a high-percentage pass or shot to either side.

4. FORCING DRIBBLER TO USE WEAK HAND

Few dribblers can drive with their weak hand as effectively as with their strong hand. By overplaying the dribbler's strong hand, your player forces the opponent to dribble with the weak hand.

Again, your players should overplay the dribbler by taking a position a half-body to the dribbler's strong-hand side, with your forward foot outside and back foot aligned with the middle of the dribbler's body.

Employing The Press
By Robert Lehman

TYPICAL SITUATION. Your team is trailing in the final seconds of a game. You need the ball.

You need to cut your team's deficit by getting defensive stops and easy scores. The best way to achieve that objective and realize victory is to defensively press an opponent. This is only one situation in which a press is effective.

A press can be used to control or to change the tempo of a game at any time. The benefits of the press go much deeper than mere strategy, though. You can see improvements in the quality of your bench, how your other defenses work and how your team is perceived by fans.

PRESS FOR POINTS

The most common time to use the press is near the conclusion of a game. The press allows for quick, high-percentage shots. It is an effective strategy, yet it does have drawbacks.

Mainly, if the press is not correctly executed, your opponents will score the easy baskets. Second, the press must be employed with enough time left in the game to score the needed points to secure a victory.

Often, we wait too long to press and find ourselves yelling, "Foul, foul." We are always wishing for just one more minute after time has expired.

It is also important to use the proper press, which is dictated by the personnel of your team and the opposition. A man-to-man press is best executed by teams with speed and quickness. It is most effective when facing a poor ball-handling team.

If your team is better described as one with size and power, a zone press would prove more beneficial. When facing a team with high-quality guards, a zone press would force the guards to pass rather than dribble the ball up the floor. This obviously takes away one of the strengths of a quality guard.

PRESS EARLY

Pulling out a game in the waning moments is not the only use of the press. Causing a few quick turnovers and jumping out to an early lead by pressing at the beginning of a game can not only settle your team's nerves, but it can intimidate the opponent. This advantage can then be exploited throughout the game.

Opponents who may be inexperienced, poorly conditioned or unable to handle the ball are all susceptible to a solid press at any juncture of the game. Also, when an opponent is slowing the tempo of the game to expose and exploit a weakness in your team, the use of a good press can speed the tempo back up to a desired level.

The effects that a pressing defense have on a team go beyond that of game strategy. A pressing team is well-conditioned from player 1 through player 12. This comes from working the press extensively in practice. Conditioning allows a coach the luxury of a deep bench. Therefore, the coach can substitute without much worry as to how a sub will perform in the game due to the strong conditioning.

The press also teaches anticipation, an asset on the defensive end of the floor. Therefore, a team's defense becomes more effective through the use of the press.

A pressing team is an exciting team, a team that fans love to watch because there is a lot of scoring.

Fan support is not essential in any way to a team's success, and should not be a factor in devising your team's philosophy. However, fan support does make it easier to want to play and gives a team concrete inspiration to work.

FIT PRESS TO TEAM

Employing some sort of press, whether man to man or zone, can be an effective tool to win basketball games. This depends on quite a few factors, though.

You must be using presses that your team can execute and use to exploit an opponent's weaknesses. Also, the press must be used in game situations that will enhance your team's chances for a victory.

All in all, pressing is a high-risk strategy. The payoff has the potential to push your team to great heights. On the other hand, it could hold a team back to the same degree. All the nonstrategic benefits are great to have, but you have to make all of the conditions favorable to prosper from the press.

> "All great teams have
> two things in common:
> defense and rebounding ..."
>
> —Larry Brown

Glossary of Terms

(Note: Positional descriptions can vary based on players.)

Ball handler—The player who dribbles and runs the offense.

Ball side—The side of the court where the ball is located.

Baseline—The line at either end of the court that runs parallel to the backboard. Can describe players' motion toward the baseline in offensive movement.

Block—The portion of the free-throw lane nearest the baseline.

Center—Usually the tallest player on a team.

Cutter—Player who moves off a screen toward the basket or to receive a pass.

Fast break—An offensive strategy in which a team advances the ball quickly up the court to score an easy basket.

Field goal—A successful 2-point shot.

Forward—A player who is usually tall and can shoot from the perimeter and rebound.

Free throw—A 15-foot shot taken from the foul line.

Free-throw line—A line 15 feet from the basket behind which players take free throws.

Free-throw line extended—A parallel position extended to the right or left of the free-throw line by a few feet.

Help side—Opposite the ball.

High post—The area around and near the free-throw line.

Inbounds pass—Throwing the ball in play from out of bounds.

Hook shot—Offensive set shot during which the player turns his or her body sideways and arcs a ball in the air toward the basket. Usually done by a forward or center.

Jump shot—An attempt from the floor to make a basket, usually from more than 5 feet away from the basket.

Low post—Area around the lane from the baseline under the basket to half way up the free throw line.

Man-to-man—Each player is assigned the responsibility of playing against one specific player from the other team.

Out of bounds—Outside the playing area. The area from which a pass can be made to bring the ball into the area of play.

Perimeter—Outside the free-throw lane.

Pivot foot—Offensive player must keep this foot in contact with the floor at all times when not dribbling.

Point guard—Primary ball handler in the offense.

Post—Area along the free-throw lane and halfway up the lane toward the free-throw line.

Press—When the defense extends pressure to the half-court line (half-court press), to the free-throw line (three-quarters press) or to the baseline (full-court press).

Screen—An offensive player intentionally blocks the path of a defensive player.

Screener—An offensive player who blocks the path of a teammate's defensive player.

Strong side—Side of the court where the ball is located.

Three-point line—Semicircle that runs around the perimeter of the basket and from beyond which a basket is worth 3 points.

Three-point shot—Shot from beyond the three-point line.

Top of the key—Area slightly beyond the top of the free-throw lane.

Weak side—Area of the court opposite the ball.

Wing—Area to the side of the offensive setup, usually the free-throw line toward the sideline.

Zone—When players are assigned a certain area to play instead of a certain player to play.

Chapter 2

Full-Court Defense

Simple, Effective Full Court Zone Press
By Peter Harris

ESTABLISHING A GOOD full court press should be an integral part of every coach's game plan. It can be used anytime during the game to gain momentum or to spark a comeback.

We've used this particular press for 5 years with great success. It's simple to teach and fun for the players.

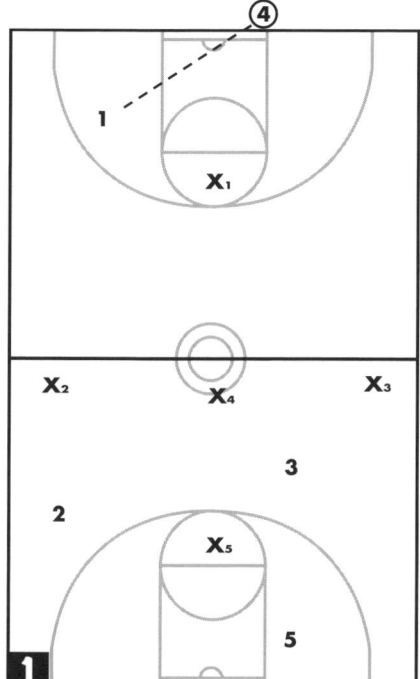

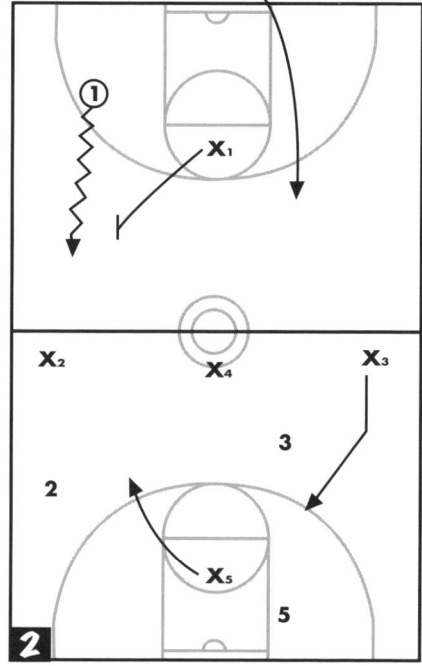

Full-Court Defense 29

Diagram 1: This is the basic setup. X1 should force 1 into a double team trap along one of the sidelines by keeping pressure on the ball. X2, X3 and X5 rotate simultaneously depending on which way 1 dribbles. X5 is considered the "safety" position. X4 must be an intelligent player able to make good decisions quickly.

Diagram 2: X1 forces 1 to the right. X2 prepares to double team as X5 rotates and anticipates a lob pass to 2. Since X5 has left the basket open, X3 must rotate to fill the safety position. X4 must read the play and anticipate a pass to either 3 or 4.

sprint and follow the pass. However, sometimes X1 is too far away to make it, so X4 and X1 switch roles. X4 and X3 create the double team, X1 covers the middle and X5 rotates to the ball side and X2 becomes the safety.

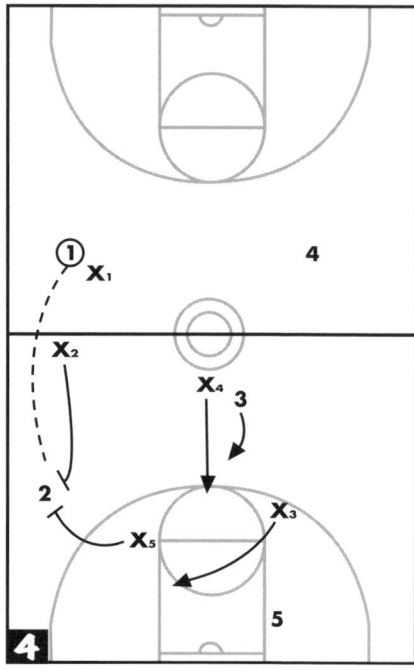

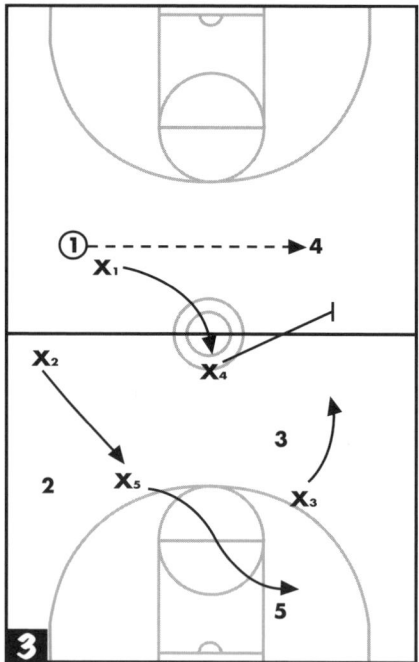

Diagram 3: If 1 sees the trap coming and reverses the ball with a pass to 4, ideally we'd like X1 to

Diagram 4: If 1 completes the pass to 2 before X5 can deny it, X2 and X5 create the double team. X1 and X4 move into positions to deny 1 and 3.

Diagram 5: If X1 cannot force 1 to dribble toward a sideline, X4 creates the double team with X1. X2 drops back to deny 2, X3 drops to deny 3 while anticipating a pass to 4.

Diagram 6: If 1 completes the pass to 4, X1 follows the pass to create the double team with X3. X4 stays to deny the reversal pass. X2

TIPS FOR A BETTER ZONE PRESS

1 The ideal place to create the double team trap shown in diagrams 1 to 6 is just past the half-court line. After the offense crosses, the line acts as a third trapper. It's even more effective the closer you get to the sideline.

2 When a point guard is forced to one side, they often try to beat the press by speeding down the sideline. In this situation, defenders X2 and X3 should plant their outside foot so it touches the sideline. We've drawn charges by doing this.

3 Always stress to your players that a press is a gamble. You may get a steal or turnover, but you may give up an easy basket. Minimize the latter by teaching your players when to apply pressure and when to retreat. Remember, it's OK if they "break" the press, just don't let them "beat" it.

4 For a zone press to be effective, players must have confidence and trust each other to do their respective jobs. When players don't feel the freedom to trap and deny passes, the press loses its aggressive edge. Always communicate with each other.

5 An effective way to sharpen the press is to make a game out of it during practice. We divide our players into two teams and take turns throwing the press at each other while keeping score. The defense gets 1 point for every turnover. The more you practice trying to break it, the better you get at executing it.

rotates to deny 3 while X5 denies the pass to 5.

Full-Court Defense

Run & Jump: Applying Defensive Pressure All Over The Court
By Don Horwood

THE RUN AND JUMP is a very aggressive man-to-man pressure defense. In this defense, pressure can be applied all over the court, and it becomes very difficult for teams to execute their set offense or press break. This defense grew out of a full-court man-to-man press that forces the offensive team to dribble the ball up the court. We felt that once the ball was put on the floor, there would be opportunities to trap the ball handler.

This defense is an organized attack, even though at times it seems disorganized. The big advantage this defense offers is that the offense never knows when or if the trap will come; therefore, it's difficult to prepare for it. Because it's a man-to-man defense, a player is always responsible for their own assigned player, plus get in position to help a teammate. Pressure can be applied all over the court, so there's no time for the offense to rest. This defense puts constant physical and psychological pressure on the offense.

The Run & Jump defense has been very successful for us for several reasons:

✔ Our players really enjoy playing it. They now run and jump even in pickup games.

✔ Good man-to-man pressure is more difficult to operate against because it requires the offense to dribble. Even if you have good ball handlers, the traps make your poorer players dribble the ball because they have no one to pass to until they start to dribble.

✔ It forces the offensive point guard to work extremely hard, and the constant pressure can wear the opponent down late in the game.

✔ With the exception of the guards, each player must recover to their own assigned player after a trap attempt. Therefore, there is less confusion on defense.

✔ Because it's not a set defense-such as 2-2-1 zone, for example-it can be run from any alignment at any time.

TEACHING PROGRESSION

The Run & Jump defense can be a very successful one to implement. However, it does take a lot of time to teach it. The following seven drills comprise a teaching progression that has worked for us:

1. Defend the Dribbler-No Hands.

Diagram 1: This is a 1-on-1 full-court defense drill in which the

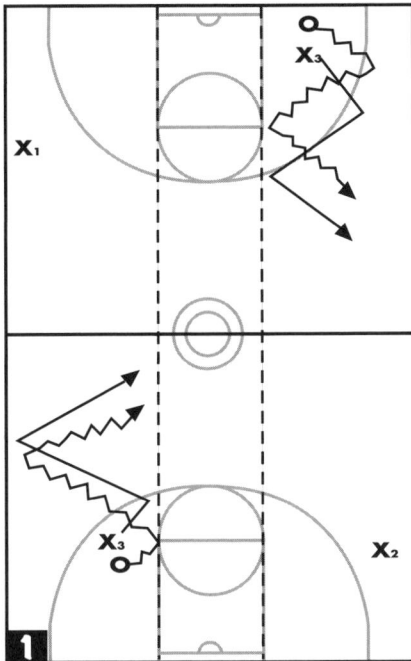

defenders (X) are not allowed to use hands. The court is divided into two outside lanes (A and B) that are bounded by the freethrow land on one side and the sideline on the other. The defender must put both hands behind the back and rely on footwork to defend the dribbler. The object here is for the defender to force the dribbler to either side of the lane and then turn. The dribbler does not try to beat the defender in this learning stage.

2. Defending The Dribbler-Hand Position.

This is the same drill as above, except now the defender must emphasize proper hand position. We want the defender to have the lead hand up and the back hand down, so that when the defender gets in front of the dribbler, the dribbler must change direction. By keeping the back hand down, if the offensive player tries to cross the ball over in front of their body, the defender is in position to get the ball without having to lunge. This forces the dribbler to turn their back whenever they change direction. The offensive player must cooperate in this learning phase, as well.

3. Live One-on-One.

Again, this is the same drill, only now the dribbler tries to beat the defender. The defender here must learn to turn and run if beaten. The defender must regain position and work to turn the dribbler as quickly as possible.

4. Two-on-Two Full-Court.

There are three offensive rules in this drill:
A. No long passes.
B. The player without the ball must be parallel to or behind the ball handler.
C. As soon as the non-ball handler receives the pass, they can dribble.

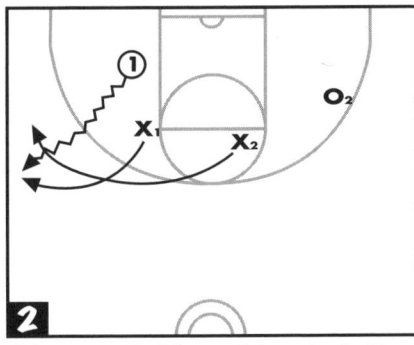

Diagram 2: Player 1 has the ball and defender X1 forces the dribble to the sideline. X2 is in the help

position. When X1 gets 1 to the sideline, the defender turns 1. X2 then comes to trap with X1. Defenders X1 and X2 must stay with 1 until 1 picks up the ball.

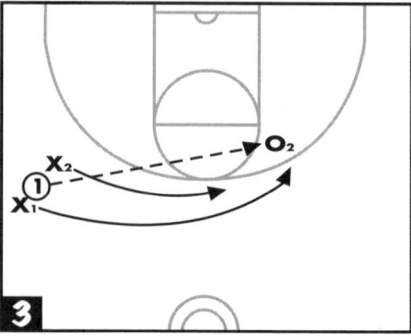

Diagram 3: When 1 does, X1 switches with X2 and goes to check 2. 1 passes to 2, and X2 must now force 2 to the sideline and turn. They continue up court until the defense gets a steal or causes a turnover. At the other baseline, they turn and come back, with the defenders on offense. *Note:* As X2 comes to trap, try to jump as high as possible to discourage the pass from 1 and 2.

5. Three-on-Three Full-Court.

In this drill, the offense has the same rules as for two-on-two.

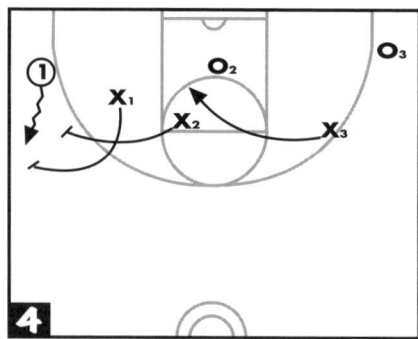

Diagram 4: Here, 1 has the ball

and is forced wide and turned by X1. X2 then comes to trap and X3 must rotate to intercept a pass to 2.

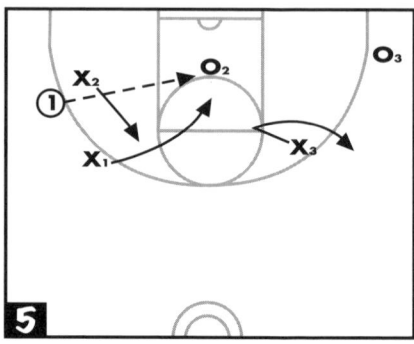

Diagram 5: If X3 cannot get there to intercept the pass to 2, the defender must fake at 2, trying to hold until X1 can get there.

Now player 2 has the ball, and dribbles toward 3, X3 must get into position to help X1, who's guarding 2.

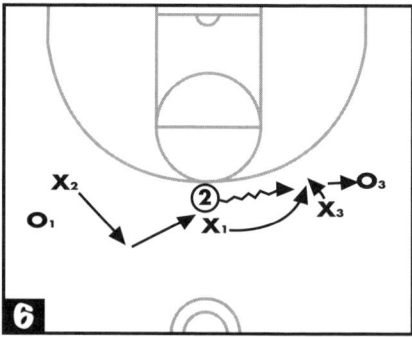

Diagram 6: By faking at the dribbler, X3 can assist X1 in turning the opponent back to X2. When X1 turns 2 back to X2, defender X2 comes over to run and jump with X1. They continue all the way down the floor until the defense causes a turnover or they get to the endline. If the defense steals, they try to score. Defense now becomes offense and the drill continues.

6. Four-on-Four Full-Court.

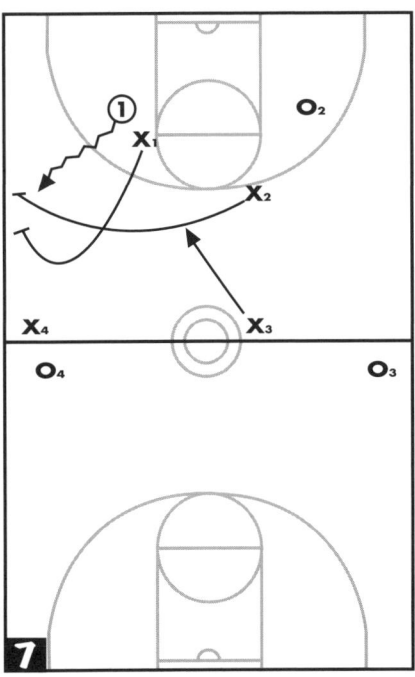

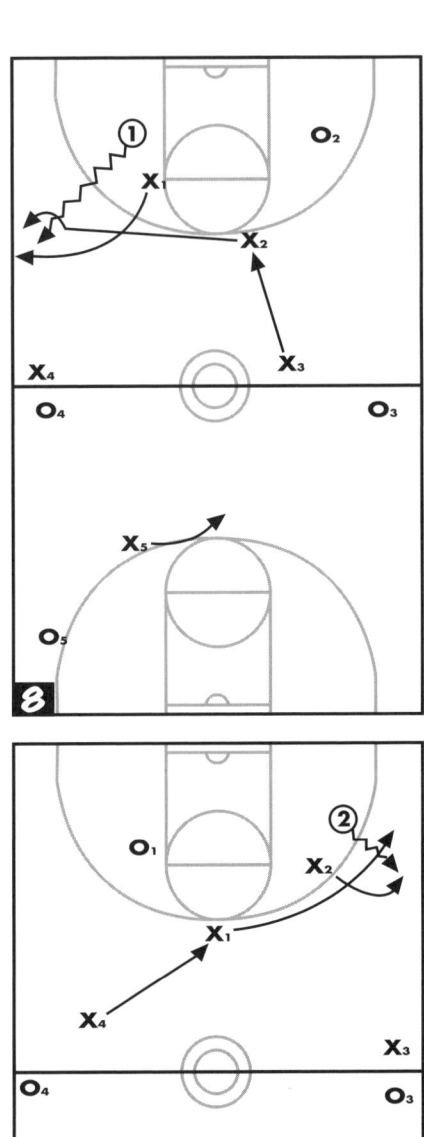

Diagram 7: In this drill, the alignment more closely resembles a game situation. The two guards are 1 and 2, and the two forwards are 3 and 4. 1 has the ball and is being pressured by X1. When X1 turns the dribbler, X2 comes to trap. X4 must stay in the passing lane. X3 must rotate up to take 2 and intercept a possible pass.

7. Five-on-Five Full-Court.

Diagram 8: This shows the proper rotation as 1 dribbles the ball toward X4. The situation is the same as in diagram 7, except that the defensive deep player must rotate toward 3.

Diagram 9: If the Run & Jump were being executed in the opposite direction, X5 would rotate 4.

Full-Court Defense

"The Hawk"—A Swarming Press That Keeps Offenses At Bay
By Willie J. Banks

"THE HAWK" IS a great press to use when you want to surprise your opponent. It's different from most full court presses since "The Hawk" puts all five players where most offenses want to break the press: lane one or the middle of the court.

Presses usually put one defender over the ball and the other four in different areas, depending on the press. Instead, "The Hawk" tries to give the look that the sideline is wide open.

X1 and X3 have to move quickly to the ball and trap. X2 is the free safety and tries to intercept the pass back to lane one. If the ball is dribbled or passed out of the trap, X1 and X2 sprint to set another trap on the ball. X3 then switches to the free safety position. X4 has ball side responsibilities. That player is responsible for any opponent from the half court line down to the baseline on the defensive side. X5 is responsible for any player going to the basket.

If the ball is skipped from one side of the court to the other, X4 and X5 stay with their defensive responsibilities. Once the ball crosses half court, move into a man-to-man. When in "The Hawk," don't allow the offense to relax for a second.

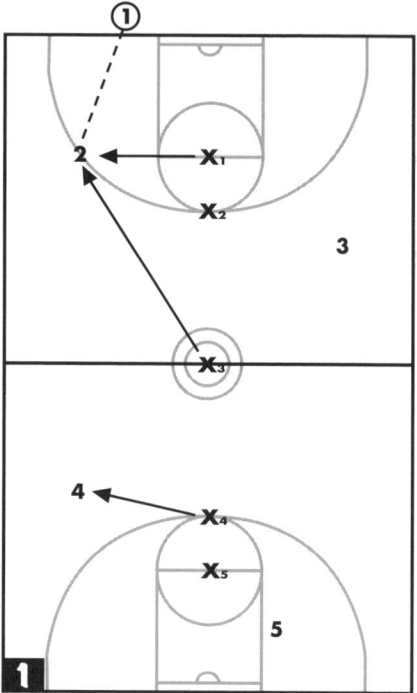

Diagram 1: Defenders are positioned in the middle of the court (lane 1). They can set up in a full or three-quarter press.

Diagram 2: X1 and X3 are the keys to the trap. When the ball is passed to either side, X1 and X3 must trap the ball. X2 plays safety and looks for a steal. X4 guards a ball side player and X5 guards the weak side.

Diagram 3: If the offensive player passes across the court, X1 and X2 will now trap and X3 will rotate to

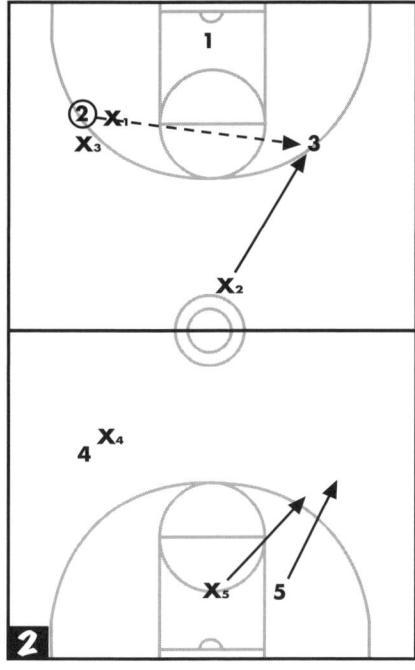

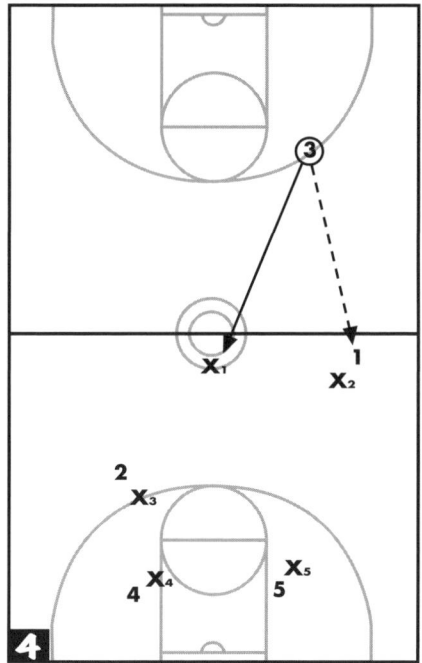

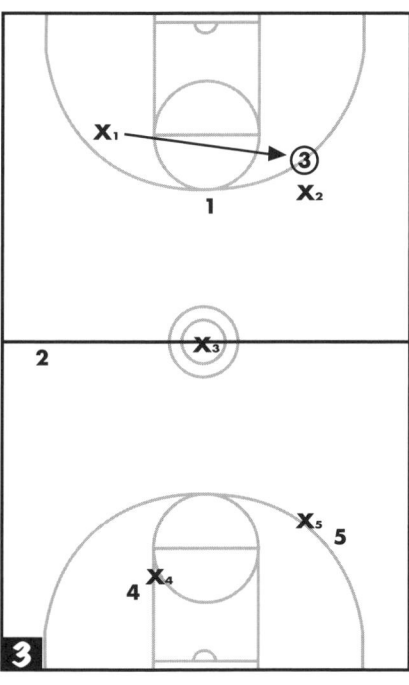

the middle. X4 and X5 will guard their opponent in the assigned area.

Diagram 4: Once the ball crosses half court, your players must know what defense they are in.

Use "The Hawk" early and late in your games. It surprises opponents because most teams have never seen this formation. You don't have to have the greatest athletes, but you should review with your team how to trap, proper foot movement and positioning.

Try not to use it too often, as with any other press, the offense will eventually break it. But if your team picks and chooses the right spots, "The Hawk" will disrupt your opponent and lead to many forced errors.

Full-Court Defense

1-1-3, Full-Court Press
By Ed Webb

THE OBJECTIVES OF the 1-1-3, full-court press are to press the ball as it approaches the three-quarter-court area, double-team the ball, cut off passing lanes adjacent to the ball, stop penetration by guards and force the opponent into making errors.

Defenses should avoid committing fouls, stop layups and force the offense into taking outside shots.

The press is not necessarily attempting to steal the ball. It is trying to force errors such as 5- and 10-second violations, bad passes and traveling to disrupt the offense.

PLAYER POSITIONS

X1. Positioned at midcourt ready to front any opponent.

X2. Positioned at the foul line ready to force the ball to the sideline and eliminate a guard-to-guard pass.

X3. Positioned at top of the key ready to cover the sideline or protect the basket.

X4, X5. Positioned three steps in from the sideline at the hash mark ready to cut off a pass up the sideline.

PLAYER RESPONSIBILITIES

X1. Must deny a pass to the middle of the floor; cover the weak side on a pass reversal (ball crosses hash mark); follow double-team rules; and take away ball reversal out of the double-team.

X2. Guide the ball up the sideline using bluff and retreat tactics; eliminate cross-court, guard-to-guard pass; deny a pass to the middle of the court when 1 covers the weak side (ball crosses hash mark); double-team in front of 4 and 5 at half court; and prevent the dribble back to the middle of the floor while not allowing the ball handler to split the double-team.

X3. Protect the basket when the ball is in the backcourt; cut off the sideline on the ball side; if the ball

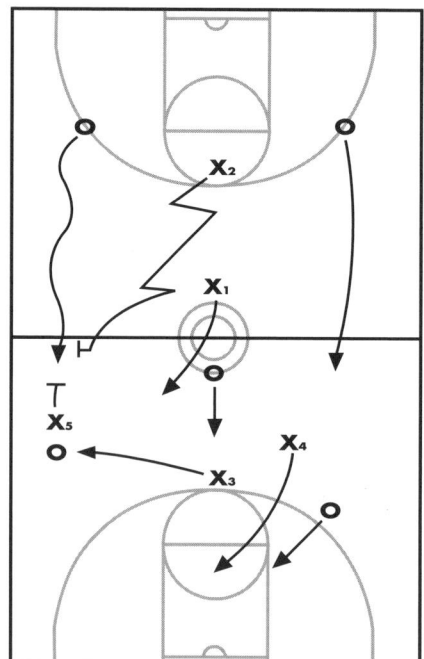

Strong-Side Coverage

is reversed, rotate back and protect the basket.

X4, X5. On the ball side: Double-team the ball as it crosses midcourt and prevent dribble up the sideline and a potential split of the double-team; retreat to the basket in the passing lanes if the ball is passed up the sideline.

On the opposite side: Rotate into the lane and protect the basket; circle out and contain if the ball is reversed; and take away any long cross-court passes out of the double-team.

DIVIDE COURT INTO 3 SECTIONS

Area 1: Gamble with X1 and X2 (anything goes).
Area 2: Be cautious. Make sure basket is protected and X3 is the only player taking huge gambles.
Area 3: Everyone covers the basket.

ADVANTAGES OF THE 1-1-3
(A Variation of the 2-2-1)

✔ It provides a different look to the offense.
✔ Chances can be taken with X1, X2, X3 or your quickest player.
✔ If the defense misses the ball, the offense can't advance the ball with a mismatch.
✔ X4 and X5 positioned on wings always allows a player to protect the basket.
✔ Starting X5 on left side allows for protection of the basket since many teams reverse the ball before crossing half court.

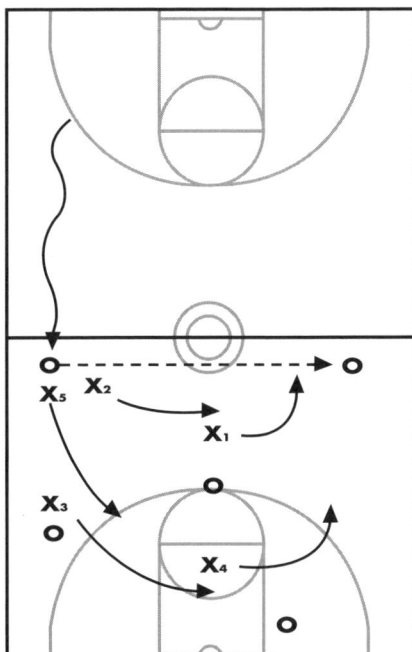

Reversal

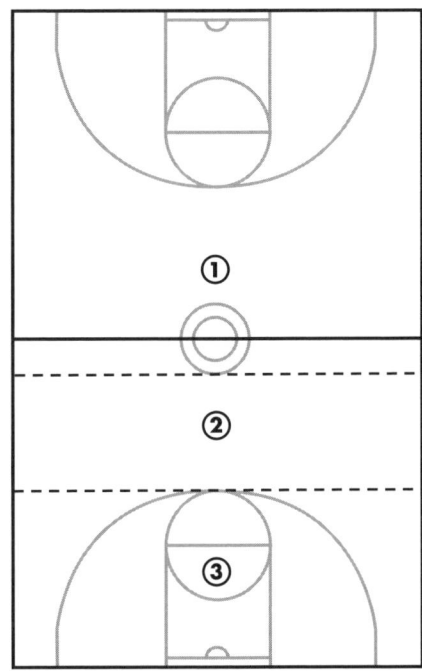

Dividing Into 3 Sections

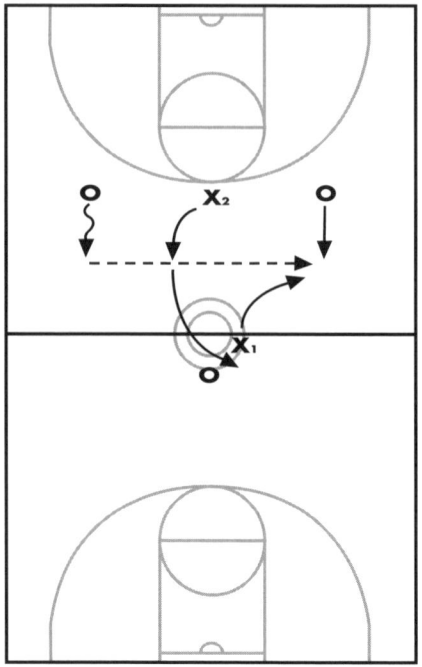

Key Note: **X2 and X1 Must Match**

When the ball crosses the hash mark in the backcourt on a guard-to-guard pass, X2 and X1 must switch assignments.

Diagrams represent coverage schemes which can be used as drills in practice.

Diagram 1: Three-on-two, two and one coverage.

Diagram 2: Two-on-two strong side.

Diagram 3: Three-on-two strong side. X3 is the interceptor.

Diagram 4: Three-on-four strong side. Concentrate on weak side protecting the basket.

Diagram 5: Four-on-five. Concentrate on stopping pass to middle and force ball reversal.

Diagram 6: Reversal. X1 anticipates cross-court pass and back

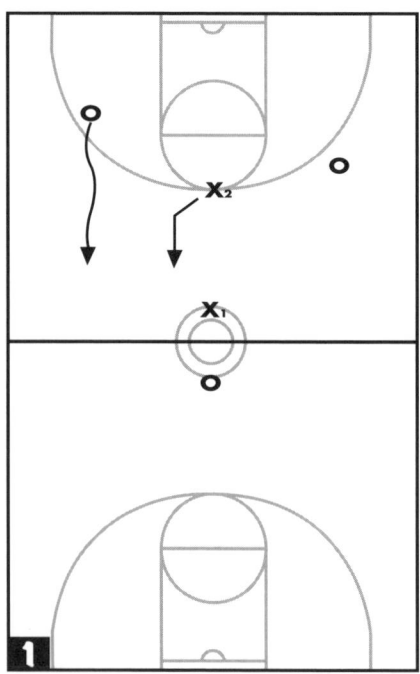

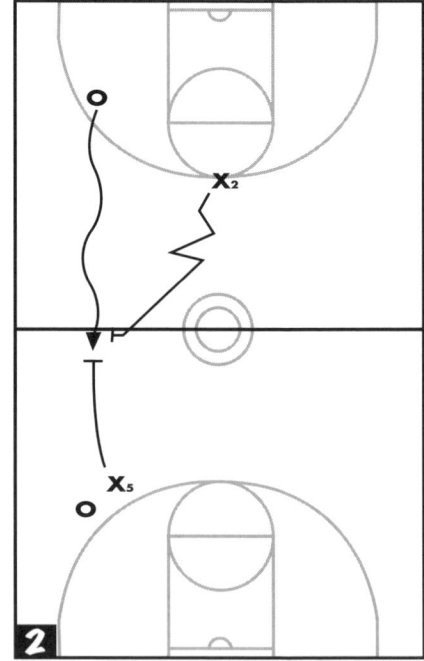

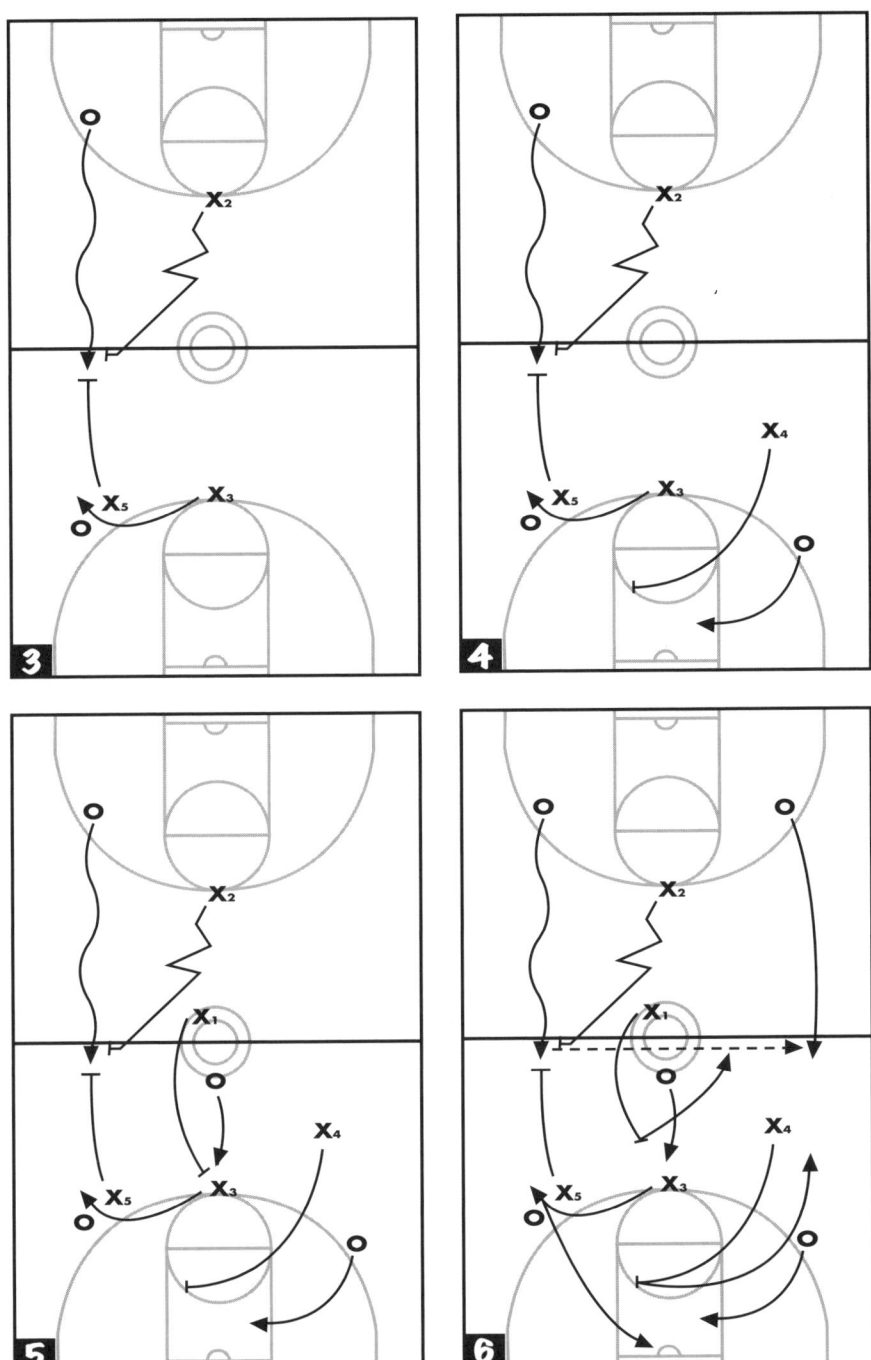

Full-Court Defense

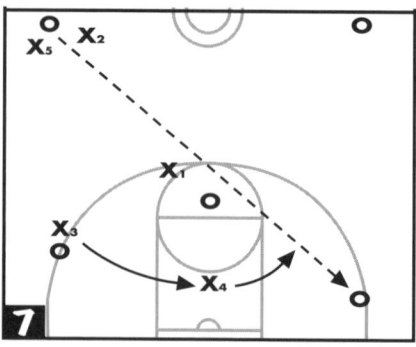

defenders rotate and protect basket.
Diagram 7: Back defender must look for a long interception.

How To Run The 1-2-1-1 Zone Press
By Ed Webb

IT"S VERY IMPORTANT for coaches to allow their players the opportunity to have fun while trying to accomplish team objectives. I've never met a player who did not want to play a fast-paced, full-court game, whether it be the fastbreak or full-court pressure, such as the 1-2-1-1 zone press.

The theory of running a pressure defense such as the 1-2-1-1 has lots of logic behind it. For example, few teams like to play against a pressure defense because it forces them to put in extra time to prepare for it. In addition, a pressure defense often becomes a conditioning test for them.

From your team's point of view, using a pressure defense can hide certain areas in which you may be weak. It also allows a coach to play more players and to control the tempo of the game. Plus, it can be a great confidence builder for your team. There are several objectives we want to accomplish with our pressure defense (taking the ball away on a direct steal isn't necessarily one of them):

1. Press the ball out-of-bounds.
2. Double-team the ball and cut off the adjacent passing lanes.
3. Stop penetration by the dribbler.
4. Force our opponent into errors (10-second violation, a bad pass, traveling, etc.).
5. Do not foul (unless the situation warrants it).
6. Stop lay-ups.

PLAYER POSITIONS AND RESPONSIBILITIES

As with any defense, the 1-2-1-1 zone press assigns certain positions and responsibilities to defenders.
POSITIONS:
Player X4: Left side of the bas-

ket tight on the baseline where the throw-in usually occurs.

Player X2, X3: One step outside the foul line extended, forcing the inbounds pass into the corners and not letting the ball handler pivot and face up when he receives the pass.

Player X1: Halfway between the top of the freethrow circle and the midcourt circle, ready to protect the strong-side passing lane.

Player X5: Halfway between the midcourt and freethrow circles to protect the basket but, more importantly, also to take away the long pass to half court.

RESPONSIBILITIES:

Player X4: *1.* Pressure the ball out-of-bounds; try to prevent the high pass inbounds. *2.* Double-team the ball on the inbounds pass in front of X2 and X3. Prevent the dribble back toward the middle; do not allow the dribbler to split the double-team. *3.* Retreat to the basket in the passing lane in the middle of the floor if the ball is passed out of the double-team past the defender. *4.* Follow the ball for another double-team if the ball is thrown over the defender's head. *5.* Chase the ball when it's being advanced to the basket.

Player X2, X3: Allow the inbounds pass to a player on their side in front of them but do not allow the opponent with the ball to pivot and face up.

On the ballside: *1.* Double-team the inbounds pass. Prevent the dribble up the sideline and the split of the double-team. *2.* Double-team the ball if it's thrown out of the double-team over and up the sideline. *3.* Get in the passing lane if the ball is thrown out of the passing lane but not past.

On the opposite side: *1.* Cut off the pass back into the middle. *2.* Double-team the ball if the pass is made to an opponent in their area. *3.* Abide by double-team rules. Prevent the pass from out-of-bounds between X2 and X3 and midcourt. Cut off the pass up the sideline on the ballside. Double-team the ball if the pass is made up the sideline out of the double-team. Stop any dribbler who splits a double-team, allowing teammates to recover.

Player X5: *1.* Protect the basket against lay-ups. *2.* Take away the long adjacent pass to midcourt.

WAYS TO PLAY THE PRESS

There are four ways to play the zone press: regular, where you allow the inbound pass; overplay, where you deny the inbound pass; double-team, where you double-team your opponent's best guard with X4 on the inbound; and rover, where X4 is open in the middle of the lane facing the ball with X2 and X3 in an overplay position. Player X4 calls out where the ball is being thrown to alert X2 and X3.

Diagram 1: Divide the court into three areas. In area 1, you can gamble-anything goes (steal in a lay-up only). In area 2, chase the ball from behind for the tap-out. And in area

Full-Court Defense

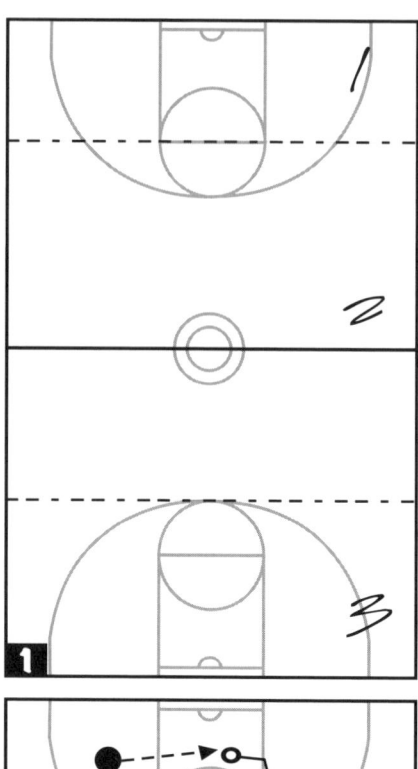

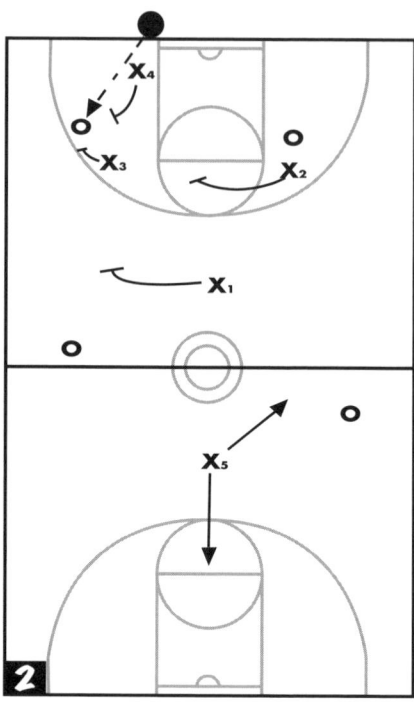

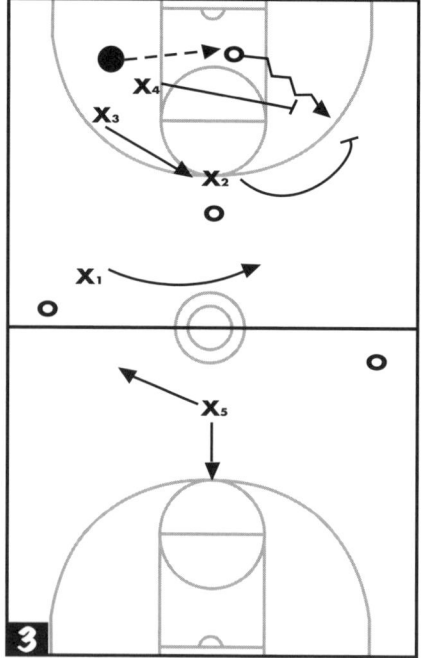

Diagram 2: Strong-side coverage.
Diagram 3: Reversal. X4 chases the ball; X2 circles out to keep the ball in front of the opponent after a 2-count, to give X3 time to cover the middle.
Diagram 4: If the ball is inbound from the side, turn the press around.
Diagram 5: A variation of the 1-2-1-1 zone press for late in the game. In this press, X2, X3 and X4 gamble. X1 and X5 protect and look for the lob pass. X2 and X3 either double or cut the middle off, and X4 always doubles. When the ball is reversed, the weak-side player circles out and gets in position to stop the ball.

To be a good pressing team, you must put your press in at the very start and allow your players to

3, sprint into the lane to make the shot come from 15 feet and out.

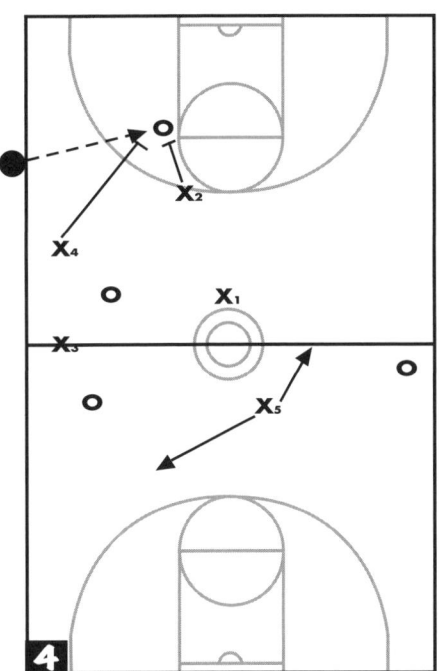
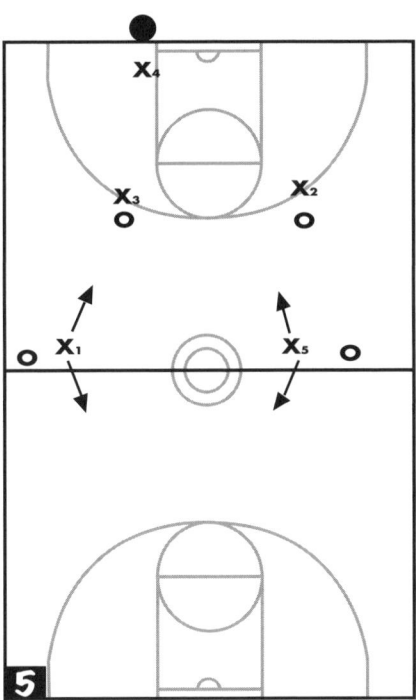

build confidence. Don't be concerned about your team's press offense at this point; there's time to work on that. But it would be discouraging to your defense if they can never experience success.

Pressure Defense As A System: The 2-2-1 Full-Court Press
By Buster Harvey

OVER THE YEARS I have watched many teams with varied levels of talent enjoy great success using pressure defense.

Outlined below is the 2-2-1 full-court press I used while coaching at various levels. Although our system included several presses at different positions on the court, the 2-2-1 full-court press was our "bread and butter" press.

BY-PRODUCTS OF A PRESS

✔ Presses are exciting.
✔ They get your team in good physical condition.
✔ Creates tempo.

✔ Creates situations.
✔ Players and fans love it.

GOALS: WHAT WE WANT

1. To force mistakes. Errors — not just turnovers (rush their offense, time outs, bad shots, etc.).
2. Set the tempo of game.
3. Offset the pace of opponents.
4. Apply constant pressure
5. Make the opposing team play 94 feet.
6. Utilize superior conditioning for the entire game.

EXECUTION, KEY NOTES

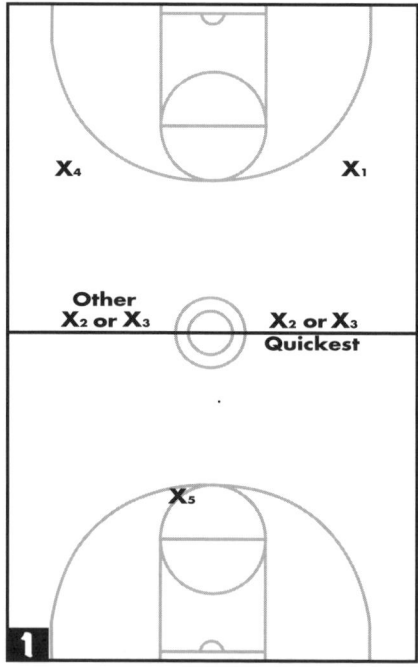

Diagram 1: Formation
✔ Use the press after a score, free throw (make or miss) and dead balls.

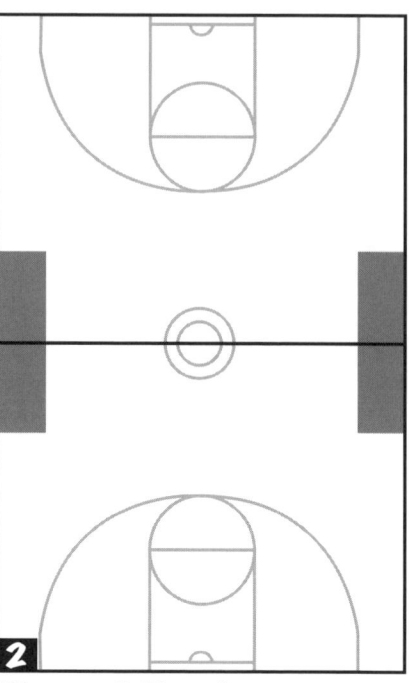

Diagram 2: Trapping areas. Force the ball to these areas.
✔ Must apply constant pressure and then retreat to level of the ball or backboard; then to half-court defense.
✔ Must dictate the tempo. Make people play your style of play. Defense dictates offense.
✔ Pressure creates mistakes and errors. Keep constant pressure and over time, it will force errors. Retreat to backboard.
✔ Must be prepared to play every spot on the court.

RULES

1. Trapping areas. Trap when the ball goes in these areas:
   A. Coverage-side.
   B. Middle.
   C. Basket (turn sideways).

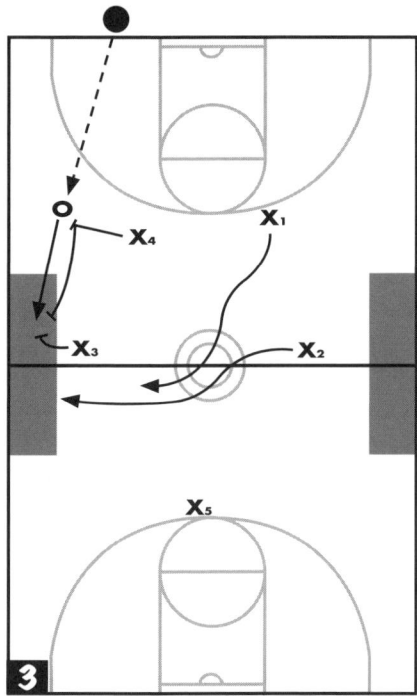

2. When the ball gets by your players, have them retreat to the level of the ball until it passes half-court — then sprint to the backboard and go to the half-court defense.
3. Stay an arms distance from the ball.
4. Apply constant pressure with your hands, use them to influence the following areas of the offense:
   - How they pass.
   - Where they pass.
5. Keep the ball out of the middle (explain to your players what happens when it goes there).
6. Don't foul.

OTHER NOTES

✔ Upon an interception, be ready to get the ball to open players and fill lanes

✔ Work on quick transitions from offense to defense and vice-versa.

✔ Allow the ball to come inbounds below the free-throw line extended (Try to step in and steal the pass on occasions).

✔ Reaching or grabbing. Pressure enough to prevent straight, sharp passes. Encourage lobs and bounce passes by using hands and being active.

✔ Do not allow anyone to dribble by your players.

✔ Direct dribbler toward the sidelines to create double-team situations.

✔ Do not reach-in to attempt to take the ball away, but have them play their position and force mistakes over a period of time.

✔ Always have your players chase the dribbler if they happen to get by and try to knock the ball to a teammate.

✔ You must have the point guard stop the ball on the dribble.

COVERAGE, ROTATIONS

A. Reverse coverages if the ball goes to the opposite side of the floor.
B. Cover side, middle, and basket areas (turn sideways to see).

POSITIONS

✔ Remember that every opponent will be different. Position your press according to your opposition's abilities.

✔ Fit the positioning of your press to your personnel.

Full-Court Defense

THE STARTING FIVE!

Get these five special basketball coaching reports for a special low price of only $13.95.

40 pages of extremely valuable coaching ideas for under 35 cents a page!

Fundamental Dribbling—
20 easy and effective dribbling tips. *8 pages.*

Nailing Free Throws—
A variety of perspectives on free throw techniques. *8 pages.*

The Recruiting Game—
Get your players ready for the rigors of being recruited. *8 pages.*

The Fab Five—
The five most popular *Winning Hoops* articles from the first 10 years. *8 pages.*

The Blackboard—
24 offensive plays with diagrams from 20 different coaches. *8 pages.*

Valued at $34.75 for the full set, these five valuable coaching reports are yours for only $13.95.*

TO ORDER, CONTACT:
Winning Hoops
P.O. Box 624 • Brookfield, WI 53008-0624
For Faster Service In The U.S., Call: (800) 645-8455 Or (262) 782-4480
Or Fax To: (262) 782-1252 • E-mail: info@lesspub.com

*Payable in U.S. Funds drawn on a U.S. bank.
Wis. residents add 5.1% sales tax.
Reports ship free in the U.S. and Canada! Foreign Postage: add $2.50 per set.

Priority Code: CHPDEF

Chapter 3

 Three-Quarter Court Defense

Running The 2-1-2 Three-Quarter Court Press
By Rob Raque

PRESSURE YOUR opponent. Create turnovers that lead to easy baskets — all without being burned by giving up open shots. The wish of every coach is to create some offense from their defense, while limiting the risks they have to take. This is a difficult, sometimes improbable, balancing act as most pressure offers a high risk/high reward.

If you want to create some easy offense through pressure, but are concerned about the chances you take in pressure defense, the 2-1-2 three-quarter court press may be for you.

My teams have encountered and solved all types of pressure with one exception — the 2-1-2. The 2-1-2 is a press you don't see that often and is hard to prepare for. It has three key benefits:

✔ It allows you to pick your spots, to take chances and remain aggressive, while keeping good protection in the defensive frontcourt.

✔ You don't need great athleticism or size to benefit from the press (although having both enhances the press's effectiveness) — therefore, it can be used at any level of play.

✔ It covers the middle passing lanes well, discouraging the most preferred and used attack against pressure.

OBJECTIVES

The 2-1-2 press does require patience and discipline, as you are letting the offense work itself into trouble by limiting available options and time for decisions. You want the offense to force their press attack by ensuring there are no clear decisions available.

SPECIFICALLY, YOUR GOALS ARE:

✔ Take the opposing offense out of their rhythm by disrupting and slowing down their press attack.

Three-Quarter Court Defense 49

✔ Force your opponent to take time off the clock in the backcourt while trying to figure out what type of press coverage you are playing, causing the offense to be timid.
✔ Force at least one of the following:
  ● A "read" mistake by the ball handler, who then takes off on an uncontrolled speed dribble up the sideline.
  ● Backcourt passes to be made late in the 10-second count, especially reversal passes to the opposite wing.
  ● Short passes into the trap zones which are more easily trapped.
  ● A trapped player to throw "window" passes (forced passes into tight openings) to the "dead-spot" area (cross-court, diagonally opposite ball) or deep sideline areas. These forced passes are the ones you must anticipate and steal.

This press is most effective against teams with strong ball-handling guards, but without other confident ball handlers. Typically, these teams rely on their point guard to extract them from trouble.

POSITION DESCRIPTIONS

Diagram 1: Front Players (X1, X2)–Usually your guards. These players must be quick, agile, patient and possess some savvy. Players out front cannot "jump the gun" and must know how to bait the offensive player with the ball. If

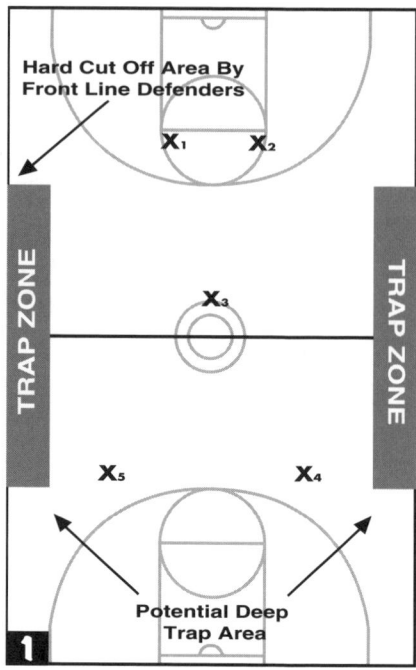

you can put players with size here, it's a huge plus!

The two players are in an inverse relationship with each other; when one steps up to influence the ball, the other must quickly drop towards the middle for help responsibility. Their pick-up point should always be a point between the free-throw line and midway into the key circle.

Middle Player (X3) — Usually your 3 or best athlete. This player is the quarterback of the press and must be quick and willing to work very hard. X3 also needs good court vision and the ability to anticipate. Above all, X3 must be patient.

Back Players (X4, X5) — Usually forwards or center. They should be your best basket protectors and very good anticipators who can read and react accurately.

DIFFERENT COVERAGES

It is imperative that you play all three coverages well. If you do not have the personnel to play each coverage, don't! Ideally, you want to play as many coverages as possible and mix them within your game plan to allow for as much confusion in the reads for the offense as possible. When run properly, they set up each other well.

Keep in mind, the main source of uncertainty for the offense is caused by trapping only at opportune times, thus the defense stays clear of giving up high percentage shots. Traps seem to occur randomly. Therefore, it isn't essential to create traps that aren't there — let them happen!

"CONTAIN"

This is the safest way to play and may or may not create a trap in this coverage.

In contain, you consciously let the offense choose its initial method of attack, then play off that choice to limit their options.

Ideally, you will bait them into

---

7 PRINCIPLES OF THE 2-1-2 THREE-QUARTER COURT PRESS

1. This press can never be dribbled through.

2. Front players must not get split, allowing the ball to be dribbled between them. One player must influence the ball to their side of the floor, but do not end up with both players on the ball.

3. All five spots must be patient. It's important to know what coverage you are playing within the press and stick with the objectives of that coverage. Players must get a feel for picking their spots to be aggressive and take chances. Again, you're relying on the offense to panic or force itself into bad situations. These traits will be helped a great deal by scouting the opponent's press attack tendencies.

4. Each player must be willing to see two players at once, splitting their vision between receivers off the ball. This will help players with anticipation and reaction abilities.

5. The coach must clearly define the coverage areas, types and responsibilities. You have room to tweak this press to situations and personnel, but you must clearly define: who has middle-pass denial responsibilities, who traps where, who plays the "dead-spot" area and who has basket protection.

6. Although you are not initiating an attack as in other pressure defenses, players must stay low and keep their feet active. They must move on the pass, not after the pass. Positioning and readiness allow you to gain an enormous advantage in creating difficult angles and reads for the offense.

7. On any pass out of or over the press, players must sprint back toward the middle of the floor, favoring the ballside and middle for protection. Once in the key and lane area, they can fan out, recover to their assigned player (if in man-to-man) or to their position (if in zone).

taking more time early in the backcourt trying to read the press, rather than trying to beat the 10 count on a speed dribble.

You may also force a ball reversal pass late (more than six seconds) in the count.

ble. X4 must be close enough to 4 to discourage another sideline pass,

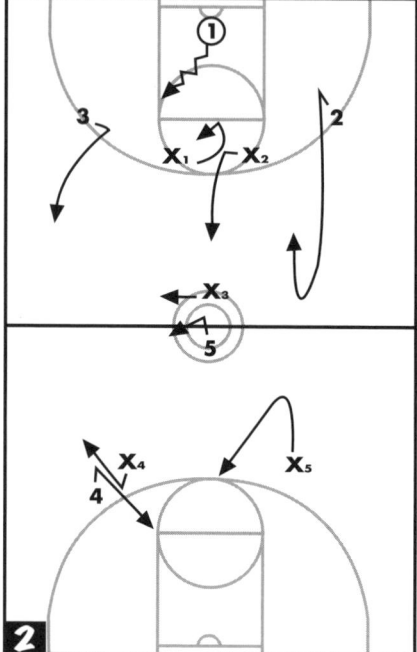

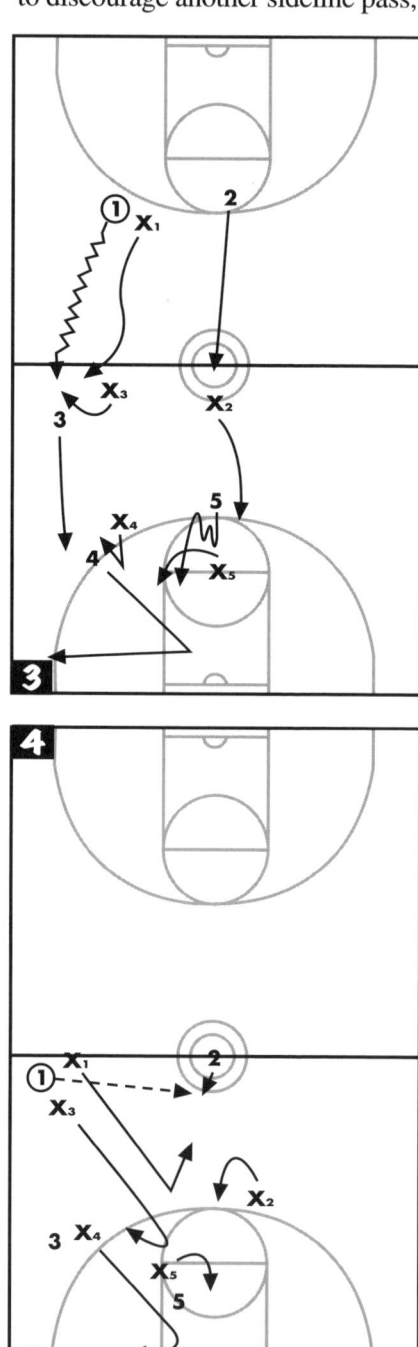

Diagram 2: X1 influences ball to one side, "giving" or yielding with the ball at a 60 degree angle to the hashmark. X2 shades the middle passing lane. X3 fronts the middle initially, then shades toward the ball-side sideline. X4 and X5 react to releasing offensive players (3 or 5) and protect the basket.

Diagram 3: If 1 continues to try and speed dribble the sideline, X3 and X1 can patiently let the trap form just over half court. X2 tries to split 2 and 5 as much as possi-

but at the same time shade towards 5. X5 bumps all middle cutters in the path to the basket.

Diagram 4: On any pass out of the trap, the defense sprints to the nearest player or drops into a zone.

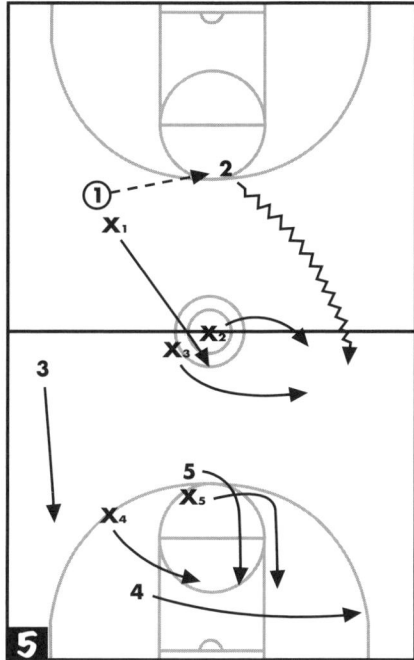

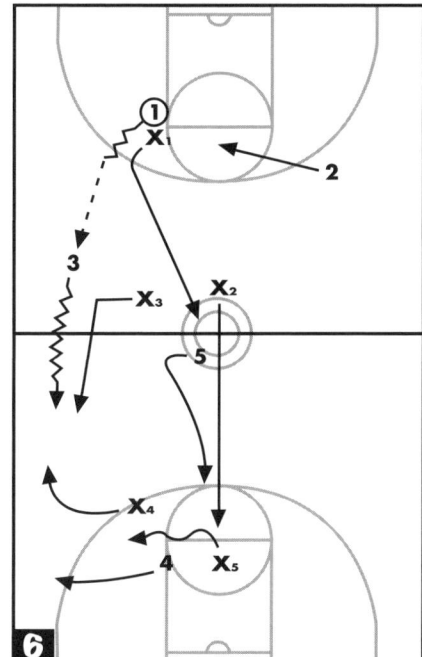

Diagram 5: If the ball is reversed, you may be able to create a trap with X2 and X3, but don't force it. X3 might be able to get there, but it is better to contain and miss the trap than to overplay and get burned.

"FORCE"

While force coverage is the most aggressive way to play, it provides the highest risks.

Diagrams 6 and 7: In Force, X1 plays hard aggressive defense on 1, initiating the early pass to 3. If 3 dribbles up the court, X2 has to hustle back to get in front of 5. The trap in force will occur deeper in the trap zone. X3 initiates the trap

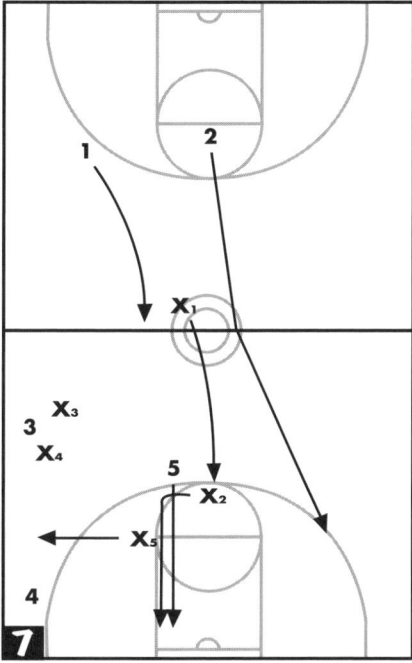

Three-Quarter Court Defense

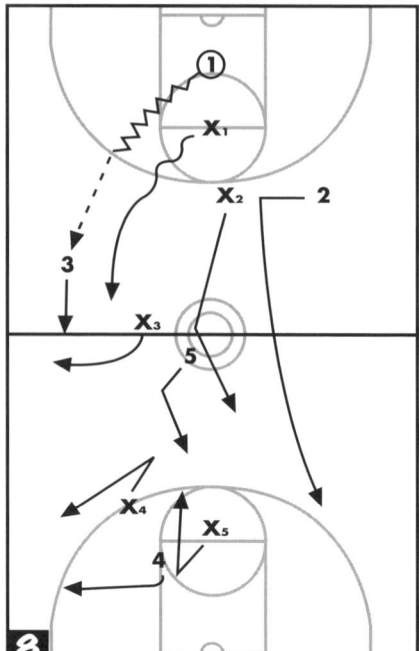

to steals and deflections, anticipating a reversal pass to 1 or 2, or a lazy pass to 5 in the middle.

"TEASE"

Tease is a combination of both force and contain coverages. While it creates the most uncertainty by the offense, it's the hardest to play defensively.

Diagram 8: X1 is very active, attacking and retreating, trying to force 1 wide with the dribble.

On a short pass (before half court) to 3, X3 gets in position to trap with X1. X2 looks to steal middle or reversal passes to 5 or 2.

X4 starts shade to corner, X5 stays in the middle. If 3 dribbles up the sideline the trap will occur deeper in the trap zone with X3 and X4 (see diagram 7).

with X4. X5 stays in the middle as long as possible, then shades the ball-side corner. X1 becomes key

---

"Defense is just hard work. There will be nights when your shots won't fall, but you can play good defense every night ..."

—Red Auerbach

The Magic 11 Defense
By Don King

IS IT REALLY MAGIC? Well, probably not quite, but the results we've achieved have been impressive. If you are interested in an effective change-up defense to complement your primary man-for-man, take a hard look at the 11.

STRENGTHS

1. You can pick up the ball at any desired point on the floor.
2. You can effectively keep the ball out of the middle of the court.
3. You have excellent basket protection.
4. It is extremely flexible. You can change-up within the defense and do many things with it.
5. It's very effective in taking the tempo away from the opponent and forcing them to react to you.

Diagram 1: This is the basic formation with a three-quarter court pick-up. We actually show this alignment and pick-up early, switching out of our man-to-man.

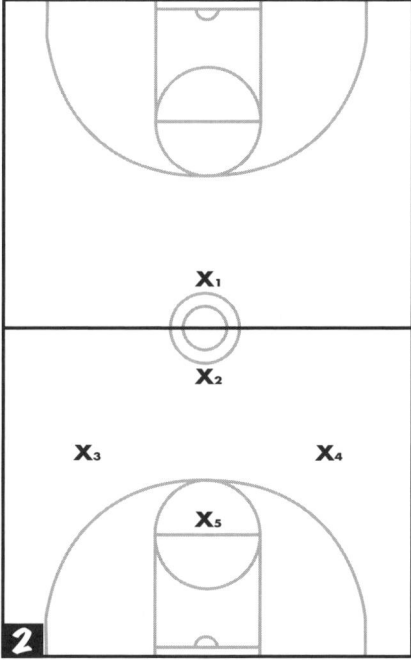

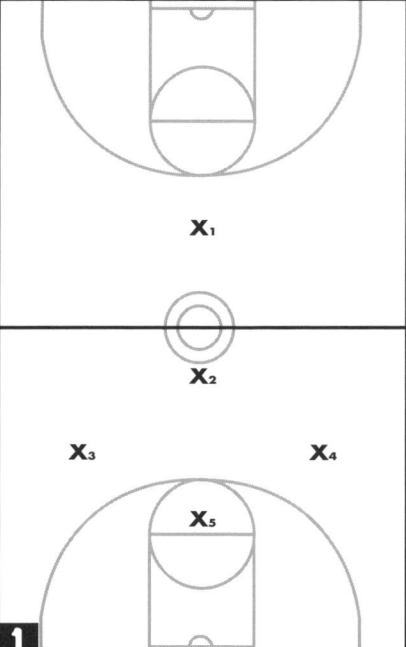

Diagram 2: After two or three plays at three-quarter court level we'll drop back to our basic 58 level, or 5/8-court. We can extend or drop our pick-up point as many times as desired during the game.

In all of our presses we teach rotating up toward the ball on the ball side of the floor and rotating back to the basket into the passing lanes on the weak side.

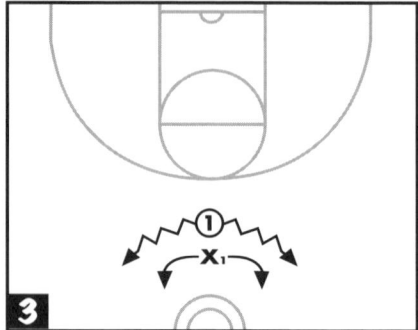

Diagram 3: In the 11 defense, X1 applies solid pressure on the ball at the pick-up point and moves the ball away from the center of the court.

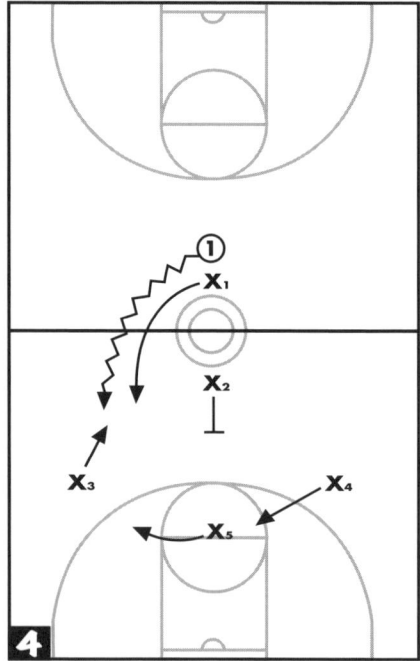

Diagram 4: If the ball comes across the center line on the dribble, X1 stays with the ball hard all the way while X2 defends the high-post area.

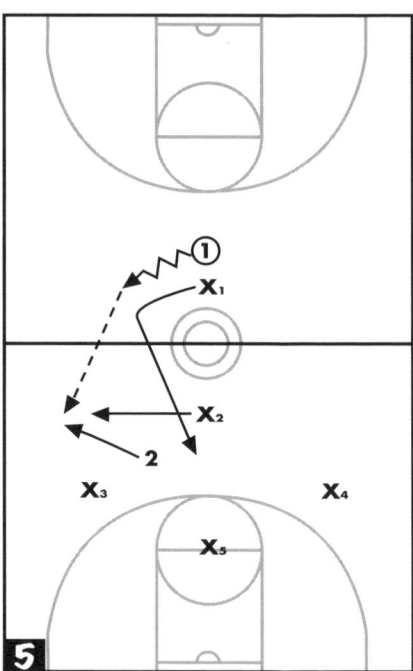

Diagram 5: If the ball comes across the center line on the pass, X2 anticipates and moves up hard to take the receiver, with X1 dropping to replace X2 in the high-post area.

We approach the opponents' sideline advance in three very distinctive ways:
- ✔ Trapping.
- ✔ Non-trapping.
- ✔ Fake trapping.

Diagram 6: We normally like to start out with very aggressive trapping by X3 or X4 with X1 just over the line in the front court.

Diagram 7: After three or four executions of hard-trapping action, we change to fake trapping and retreating by X3 and X4 in connection with one-player traps on the dribbler on the sideline by X1.

Diagram 8: We sometimes get a

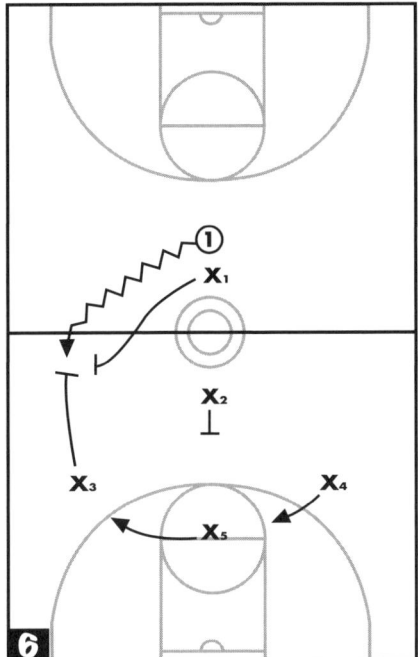

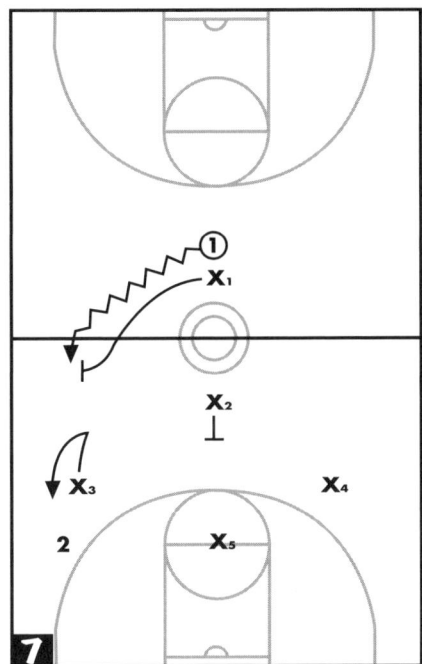

corner trap between X5, X3 or X4, although this is not a major feature of the defense.

DROP BACK DEFENSES

After penetration below the free throw line, we drop into a designated 25 (one-quarter court) defense. It can be anything and we change them up freely. It can be man-to-man, any basic zone, or a match-up or combination defense such as a box-and-one or diamond-and-one.

By altering the positioning of X3 and X4, you can change the defense significantly.

Diagram 9: By bringing both wings high we are in an aggressive 1-2-1-1 press.

Diagram 10: By anticipating and reading a predominately right-handed attack, which we experience fre-

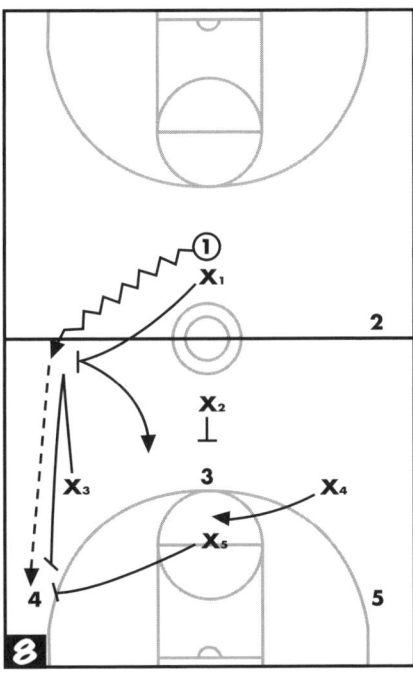

quently, we bring X3 up high and drop X4 low into a lop-sided 2-1-2.

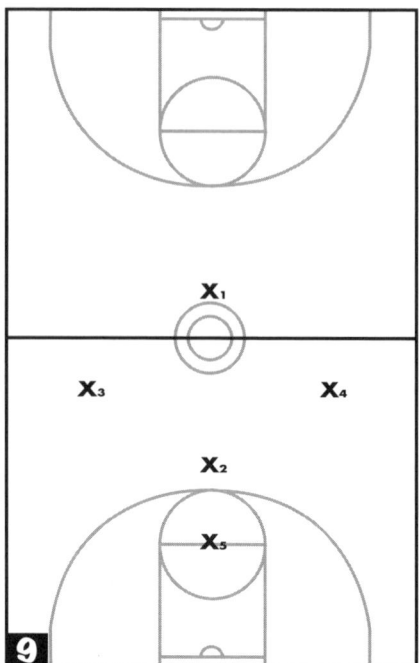

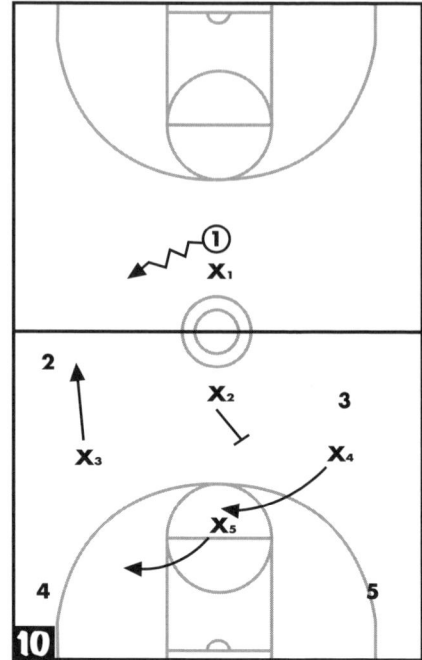

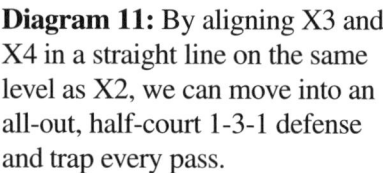

Diagram 11: By aligning X3 and X4 in a straight line on the same level as X2, we can move into an all-out, half-court 1-3-1 defense and trap every pass.

You can do so many things with this defense. We continue to teach and sell the man-to-man defense as our primary defense, but over the past five years we've incorporated the Magic 11 as a change-up defense 35 percent of the time.

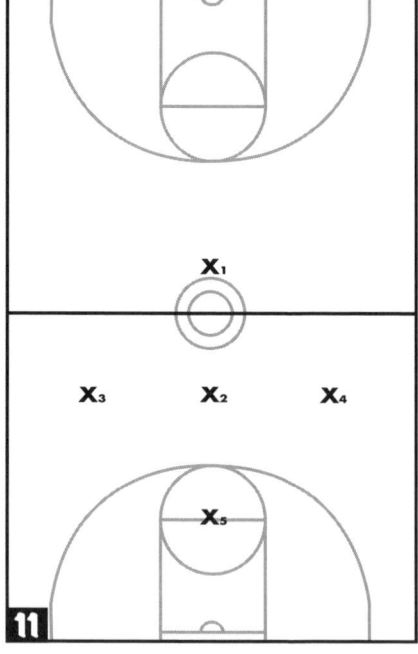

The 22 Floater...A Three-Quarter Court Press To Slow Down Good Teams
By Dick Luther

THE GREAT ATHLETIC teams, with the ability to rebound, run the break and score in many cases must be slowed down. Tempo control is what is needed in this case.

The 2-2-1 three-quarter court set can do this. Throughout the years, the 22 floater has paid big dividends for us in slowing down the pace of talented teams.

CRITICAL KEYS
- ✔ Position and quick coverage is a must.
- ✔ Keep the basketball out of the middle.
- ✔ Force the basketball to the sidelines.
- ✔ Encourage back passing and sideline-to-sideline dribbling and passing.
- ✔ Don't allow sideline penetration.
- ✔ Get back quick to set the defense when the floater is beaten.

Diagram 1: 22 Set And Movement.

22 Floater: If the basketball comes up the middle, the quickest up-defender stops the ball. Keeping the ball out of the middle is a must.

Diagram 2: Ball Toward The Sideline.

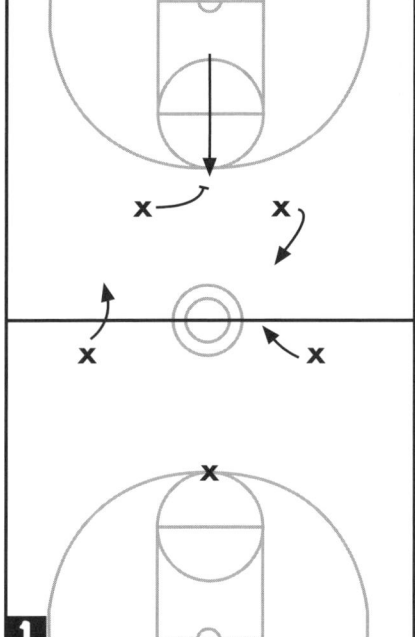

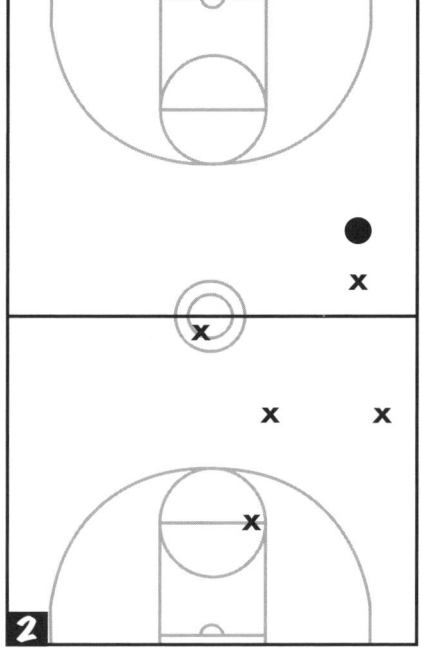

If The Ball Goes To The Sideline: Don't pressure up; instead contain. Everyone blankets the court like a huge net. Players must get big; moving arms high and low. This is not a trapping defense, it's covering floor space (containment under control).

Diagram 3: Any Cross-Court Pass (Side-To-Side). The 22 quickly switches coverage and again covers the floor.

Any Pass Ahead: The defense will scrap the 22 and quickly get back to their set defense. On our team, this means we get back to our active 2-3.

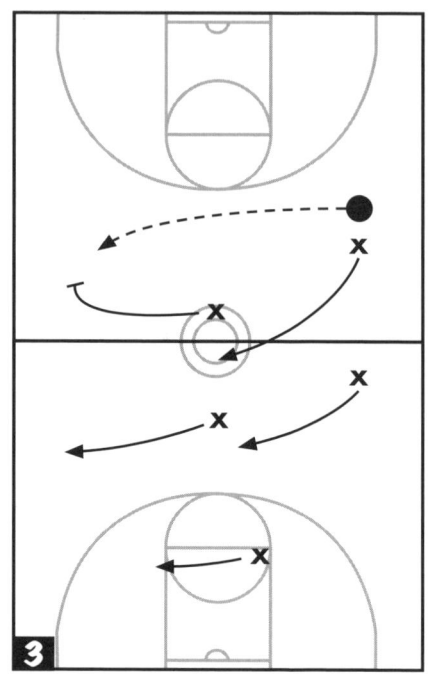

Using The 2-2-1 Dropback Zone Press/Trap
By Kevin Sivils

SINCE SO MANY teams have adopted the popular 1-2-1-1 full-court zone press and the 1-3-1 half-court trap, it's becoming necessary to find a different look defensively that the offense has not seen. The 2-2-1 dropback press may be the very weapon to add to the defensive arsenal of your team.

Diagram 1: Initial Set.

While the 2-2-1 alignment is very common, the dropback sets up about 8 feet beyond half court. This press has numerous advantages, the foremost of which is that few teams prepare to attack a defense that is initiated from that part of the court. The dropback can be extended into a regular zone press or slowly take on the form of a half-court trap.

It is possible to press off missed shots with the dropback as the defense has time to make the transition and set up, even against a fast-break team. Because few teams face such a defense, they usually attack the defense with more caution. This slows a fast-breaking team's offensive attack and causes deliberate offensive

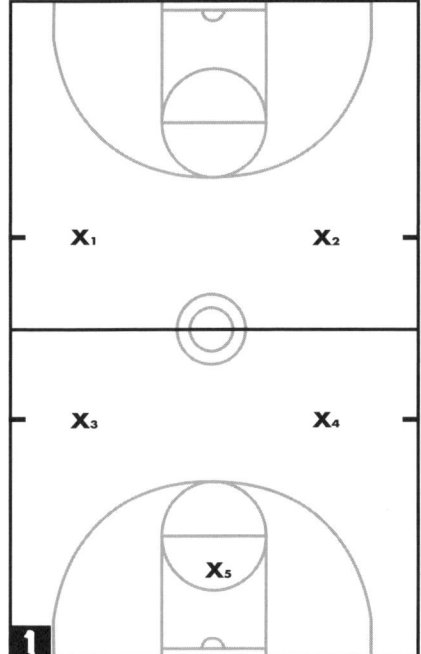

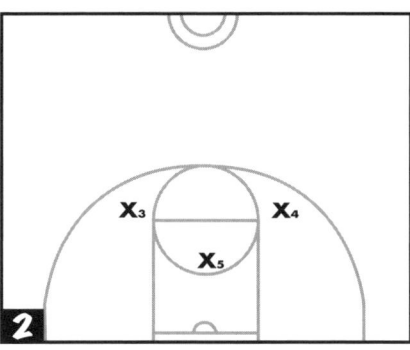

Diagram 2: Dropback.

teams to become passive and not attack the basket.

A good big player can be negated with the dropback due to the offense being forced to attack farther from the goal. This forces the post player out from the basket and away from the most effective post operating area.

USE SPARINGLY

The dropback is most effective if the trap portion of the defense is used sparingly and opportunistically. If the defense traps on every trip, the opponent will find a way to attack the defense effectively. Yet if the defense shows the dropback each trip but only traps occasionally, the opponent must deal with starting its offense from an unusual set or distance from the goal and will have trouble with the random trapping.

The dropback is also more effective if the trap comes from the side or behind the ball as opposed to the front as is traditional with the 2-2-1 set.

Trapping from the side or behind after the ball has been pushed to the sideline makes the trap more effective because the ball handler cannot see it coming and is taken by surprise. When the trap comes from in front, the element of surprise is lost and the ball handler can either pass to an open teammate or execute a pullback cross-over dribble and evade the trap. It's important to note that once the trapper has committed to trapping, the trapper must chase the ball handler until the trap is either set or the ball is passed.

GUARDS ON TOP

X1 and X2 are usually guards and position themselves 6 to 8 feet across half court or roughly at the time lines (diagram 1). Since most teams send their shooting guard to the top of the key, the point guard to half court and the other three players to the boards for floor balance, it's easier for the two guards to play these positions.

This is particularly helpful when pressing off missed shots as these defenders are in position to slow the ball's advance while the other defenders make transition. X3 and X4 position themselves roughly 6 to 8 feet across half court (diagram 1). Should an offensive player take up position in the corner, then X3 or X4 would retreat to the free throw line extended (diagram 2). X5 guards the rim and allows no one to get behind him.

Some teams use a numbered break and pre-positioning players on defense can allow them to fill their lanes quicker.

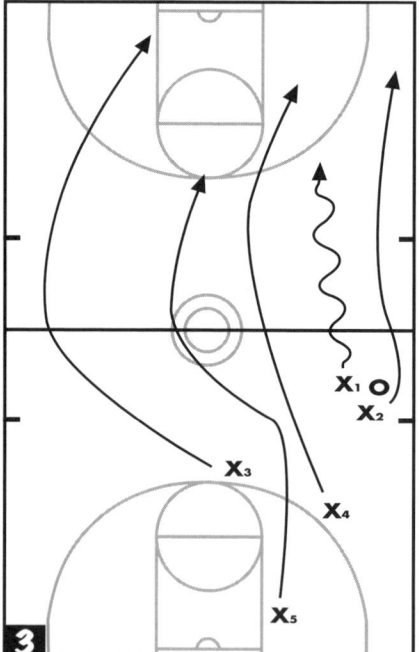

Diagram 3: X1 is the point guard, X2 runs the right lane, X3 runs the left lane and X4 posts up on the ball side for the secondary break. X5 is the designated inbounder on made baskets and the swingman on the secondary break.

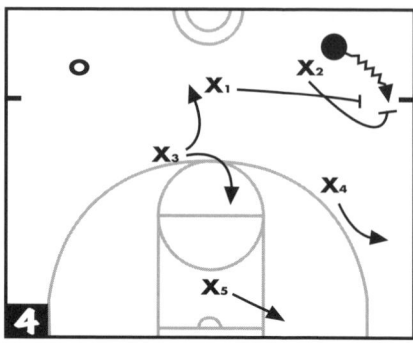

Diagram 4: Most teams attack a half-court trap with a two-guard front, a good athlete in the foul-line area and a shooter and rebounder in the corners. The dropback press covers this by channeling the ball up the sideline across half court. As X2 pushes the ball to the sideline, X1 comes from the side and traps as X2 cuts off the ball handler.

X3 covers the high post area, X4 covers the passing lane to the corner and X5 covers the rim and possible flash cuts into the low post. While covering the high post, X3 must watch the trapped ball handler's eyes and movements and anticipate a cross-court pass which must be intercepted or covered.

Diagram 5: If X3 cannot intercept the pass, he must cover the ball when it is caught. X5 now covers the pass to the corner, X1 covers the middle, X2 covers the former ball handler and X4 now guards the rim. The defense can either stay in the dropback, go to a zone defense or match up man-to-man.

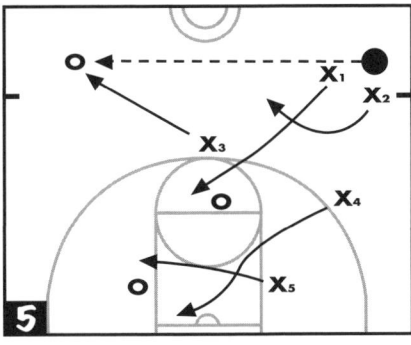

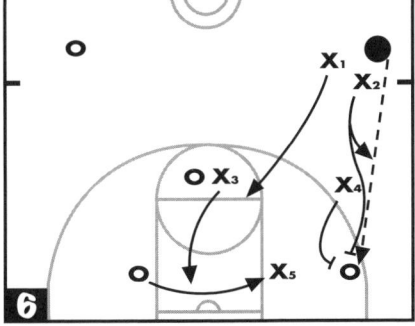

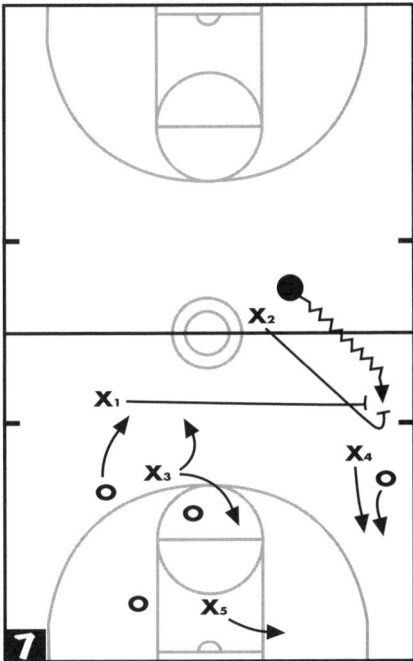

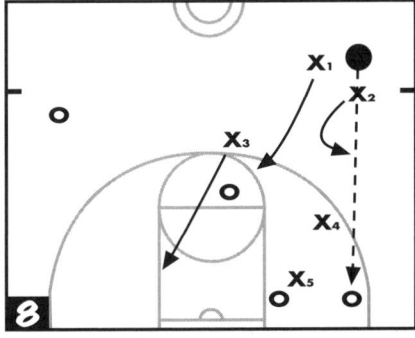

Diagram 6: If the ball is passed to the corner and X4 does not intercept the pass, X4 must now cover the new ball handler. X5 takes the ball-side low post, X3 collapses to the help side and X1 drops to cover the high post. X2 can either deny the pass out or trap. Note the defense is now in a 2-3 zone.

Should the offense attack from a 1-3-1 set, either X1 or X2 must force the ball from the middle toward the sideline.

Diagram 7: X2 has forced the ball to the sideline and X1 is coming to trap. X4 covers the forward pass down the sideline while X5 covers the ball-side low post and X3 covers the high-post area while anticipating a cross-court pass.

Diagram 8: A pass to the ball-side wing would force X4 to cover the ball, X3 to go weak side, X5 to cover ball-side low post, X1 covers the high post and X2 can again either trap or deny the pass out. The defense is again now in a 2-3 zone. A cross-court pass out of the initial trap that is not intercepted is covered with the same rotation shown in diagram 5.

Regardless of the offensive set, if the ball is successfully passed into the high post, X3 and X4 must cover it. If X3 is covering the high post and X5 and X4 are covering the blocks, X1 and X2 sprint to help pressure the ball and cover the obvious passing angles.

While it's easy to change from the dropback to a zone defense, it is also possible to change into a man-to-man defense. The easiest way is to simply match up with the offensive player in each defender's area. Should specific match-ups be desired, the defenders can be aligned so the match-ups occur naturally or the defenders can switch assignments when they're in help-side position.

The hardest way to match-up is to have the defense collapse to the lane and then pick up their assignments. This can be done, but it requires quickness, hustle and, above all, communication.

TEACH THE TRAP

When teaching the dropback press, the first skill to be taught is trapping. A two-on-one trapping drill is used with the trappers working on proper trapping technique (legs crossed forming the trap, hands tracing the ball but not reaching in, legs pressuring the pivot foot, heads and mouths communicating) and the ball handler works on beating the trap with either a pull-back cross-over dribble move or by beating one of the trappers one-on-one.

The next teaching step is to walk the defense through the various alignments and situations they could face and explain the coverages. From there, the defense plays four-on-four live with the emphasis on anticipating and intercepting passes and reading the passer's eyes and face.

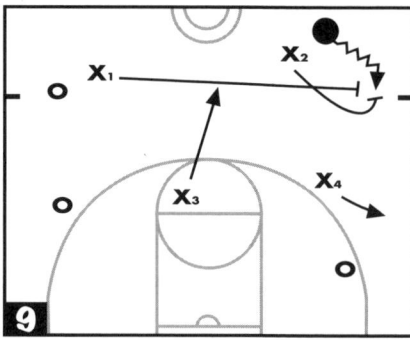

Diagram 9: The defenders must scramble back and play man-to-man defense if the pass is not intercepted. The final teaching stage is to go five-on-five live and practice the various situations in which the dropback will be used.

While the dropback press has its limitations, it can be an unusual and valuable addition to a team's defensive arsenal. It's simple, versatile, easy to learn, and requires little practice time.

Chapter 4

Half-Court Defense

Aggressive Half-Court Defense
By Steve Robinson

THERE AREN'T A lot of secrets in basketball anymore. There's too much exposure.

The key is how hard are you willing to work to get your players to implement your game plan day in and day out in both practice and in games.

If you have a team that's good on the defensive end of the court, you have a chance to win the basketball game, or at least still be in it at the end. If you can't stop your opponent, you don't have a chance.

At Florida State, our defensive philosophy is based on accomplishing four objectives:
✔ **Attitude.** Your players must develop the proper attitude about defense.
✔ **Be Aggressive.** Your players have to be aggressive with everything they do.
✔ **Challenge Everything.** Player's must challenge the shot, every pass, every dribble and their opponent's ability to get to the board for rebounds.
✔ **No Fear Approach.** Players shouldn't have any fear or doubt about what they're doing.

ESTABLISH "DEFENSIVE" ATTITUDE

The best way to instill the importance of playing with an attitude on defense is by making players aware of several tendencies or characteristics which all successful defenses have. We stress these defensive fundamentals:
✔ **Pressure The Ball.** Teach your players to work hard and put good pressure on the ball.
✔ **Get Into Passing Lanes.** Have them work hard to get at least a hand into the passing lanes.
✔ **Get A Hand Up On Every Shot.** Whether it's in the post or out on the perimeter, your players must get a hand up on every shot.

✔ **Force Mistakes.** Make the opponent play faster than what they're normally used to playing. Force them into turnovers.
✔ **Rebound.** After pressuring the ball, playing the passing lanes and getting a hand up on the shot, the play is not complete until our players have rebounded the basketball.

DRILLS TO ESTABLISH ATTITUDE

To get players to develop the proper attitude and utilize an aggressive approach on defense, emphasize defense in practice. Playing challenging defense requires hard work in drills and scrimmages. Here are several drills we run daily to get players focused on playing an aggressive, challenging style of defense.

DENY DRILLS

We work hard on denying the ball so we always have a hand in the passing lane. We want players to be in a position where they have only a hand in the passing lane and not their whole body. Stress to your players not to let the offensive player initiate contact to get open and keep them aware of the ball and their man at all times. Deny ball reversal passes and keep the ball on one side of the floor.
Diagram 1: This is poor deny positioning. To get into proper position to deny the ball and get a hand in the passing lane, the defensive player has to be on the same

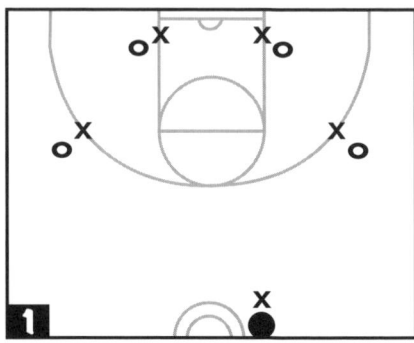

floorboard as the offensive player. Each defender must be in a good initial defensive position when the ball crosses midcourt, ready to play defense right away.

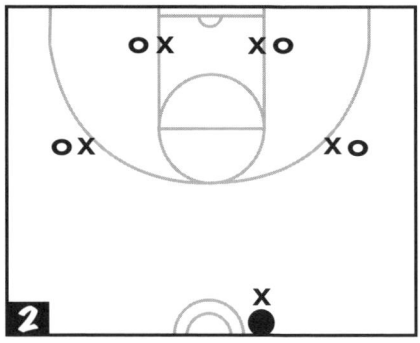

Diagram 2: Here's the proper alignment to deny the passing lanes.

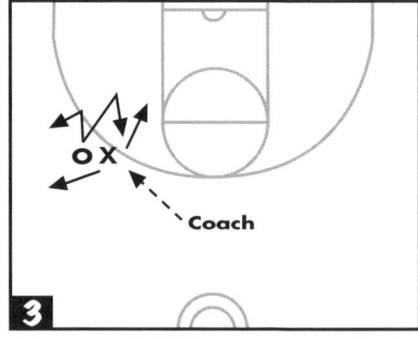

Diagram 3: This one-on-one drill with a coach is a basic drill to work on deny positioning. The offensive player works to get open for the

pass, while the defender works hard to deny them the basketball.

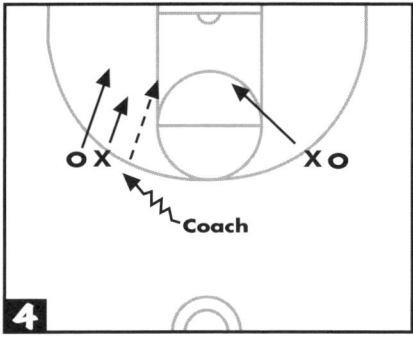

Diagram 4: The two-player deny drill is the same as the one-on-one, only this drill involves more players and gives the coach the option to go to either side. When the ball is dribbled to one side, the opposite defender can drop back and help on the backdoor cut.

JAM THE POST

When we get caught behind in post defense and the offensive player receives the ball, we "jam the post" right after the pass with double and triple teams to force the player to throw the ball back to the perimeter. Most post players are not accomplished passers, so this presents opportunities to get easy turnovers or deflections.

Diagrams 5, 6: These diagrams show how to attack and crowd the post after a player receives the ball and forces them to throw the ball back out to the perimeter.

DENY THE POST DRILLS

We make it as difficult as possible for the offense to get the ball into the post. This means fronting post

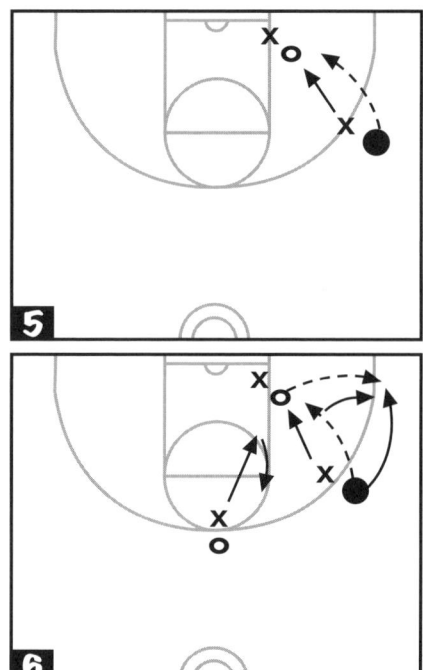

players to deny them the basketball. We want post defenders to deny the ball by getting their whole body in front of the offensive player with one hand up and one hand down. With good pressure on the ball, it allows the post defender enough time to move around in front. When played properly, the only pass that will work to get the ball into the post is a lob, which gives your back-side defenders enough time to slide over and help.

Diagram 7: This is the best drill to show post defenders the proper technique for denying the post. Position two coaches (or a coach and a player) on the wing and baseline and have the defender work on getting around the offensive player into deny position. The defender

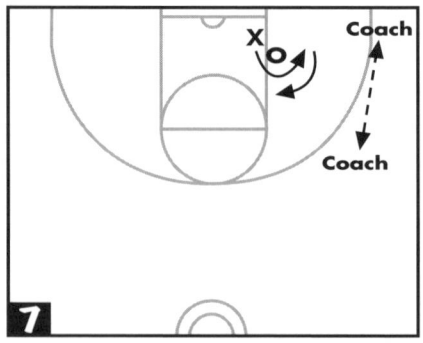
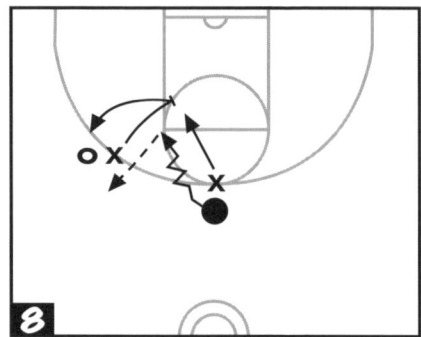

works on sliding low to high as the ball is passed back and forth on the perimeter.

SUPPORT THE DRIVE

By playing an aggressive pressure defense, it's inevitable that you are going to get beat off the dribble and defending this situation is one of the hardest things your players have to do. Not only do defenders have to be in position to deny the passing lanes, but they have to be able to slide and help on the penetration, yet still recover quickly back to their assigned player.

How you choose to stop dribble penetration will vary from game to game depending on scouting and opponent strengths. Whether you choose to bluff the help or support the drive to stop the penetration should be determined through scouting.

Diagrams 8, 9: Use these drills to support the drive to stop penetration. In both cases, the supporting defender has to work hard to slide and stop the drive, then scramble hard to recover back to their assigned player. Mix your post players with guards in these drills

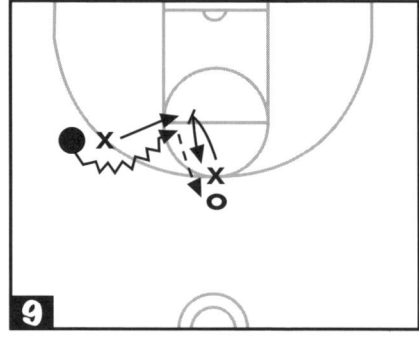
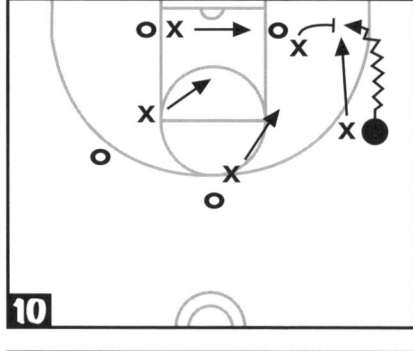
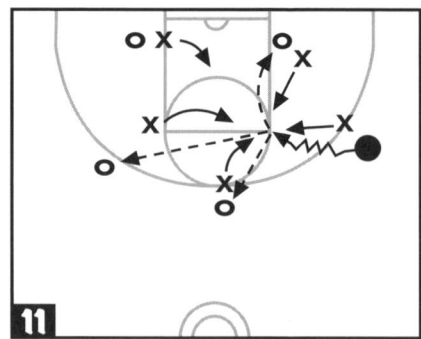

because your big players will often end up guarding a smaller player in a game.

SIDELINE DEFENSE

When the ball is on the wing, the defender should be on the same floorboard as the offensive player. Play aggressive on the ball and force the ball to the baseline and eliminate the offensive player's ability to drive the ball back to the middle. Keeping the ball away from the middle of the floor limits offensive options, optimizes the rotation and help off the dribble.

Diagram 10: Forcing the wing to the baseline allows you to be aggressive and keeps the rotation in good shape.

Diagram 11: When you allow the ball back into the middle of the floor, supporting defenders are caught in between, the rotation is less effective and the offense has multiple options.

Half-Court Man Defense
By Leonard Hamilton

IF THERE'S ONE thing that's the key to defense, it's having a system. You have to have a system that you really believe in and are comfortable with. All your assistant coaches have to believe and you have to instill into your players the belief that it will work if they think defense first.

Once the system is in place and everyone is on the same page, give your players the techniques and terminology to help them understand and execute the system effectively.

Each of your coaches must use the same terminology and stress the fundamentals of each technique to make the overall system work at peak performance.

ACCOUNTABILITY

The most important aspect after choosing a defensive system is holding your players accountable for performing the techniques to make it successful. Each player must be responsible for performing your defensive principles daily in practice and in games.

DEFENSIVE PRINCIPLES

- ✔ Closeouts.
- ✔ Contain dribble.
- ✔ Contest shot.
- ✔ Fight screens.
- ✔ Front post.
- ✔ Block out.
- ✔ Deflections.
- ✔ Sink and fill (help and recover).
- ✔ Dive on floor.
- ✔ Take a charge.
- ✔ Rebound.

These principles determine defensive success. We video tape practices and scrimmages and have a student manager evaluate and keep track of whether players are performing these tasks.

Not only is keeping these stats in practice a tool for determining defensive effort, but they are great to use in individual player meetings. If a player asks why they aren't playing more, I can say, 'You had 18 opportunities to block out in yesterday's scrimmage and you only did the job twice.' Keeping these stats is great for motivation.

THE FIVE MUSTS!

The following are things your team must do to be successful in a half-court man-to-man defense.

1. Prevent Easy Transition Baskets

✔ Take care of the basketball on offense.
✔ Sprint back and get into "attack stance and mentality."
✔ Communicate, find and stop the ball.
✔ Establish position in relation to the ball.

2. Keep The Ball Out of "Red Zone"

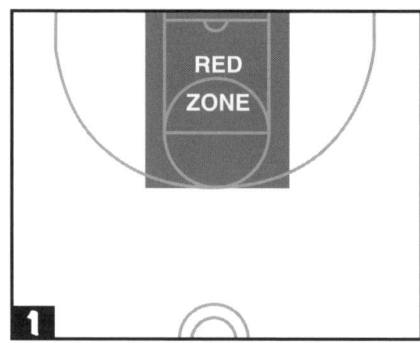

Diagram 1
✔ Prevent how the ball gets there.

✔ Stop dribble penetration.
● Pressure the ball.
● Shrink the gaps (up the line principle).
● Early help and recover.
● Execute closeouts (impair vision for a second).
✔ Take away the post pass.
● Pressure the ball.
● Front the post.
● Take away flashes and cuts.
● Swarm to help on lobs.

3. Contest Every Shot

✔ Defeat screens.
● Communicate.
● Defender guarding the screener is responsible for stopping the ball.
● "Fight like hell" when screened.
✔ Eliminate penetrate and pitch.
● Contain dribble.
● Shrink gaps (help and recover).
✔ Execute closeouts and pressure the ball.

4. Allow Only One Shot Opportunity

✔ Blockout on every possession.
✔ Eliminate penetration into "Red Zone" which weakens the block out scheme.

5. Create Offense With Defense
Diagram 2
✔ Apply pressure on the ball.
✔ Develop a "swarm to help" attitude.

OTHER KEYS TO SUCCESS

Here are other keys that translate into defensive success in the half court.

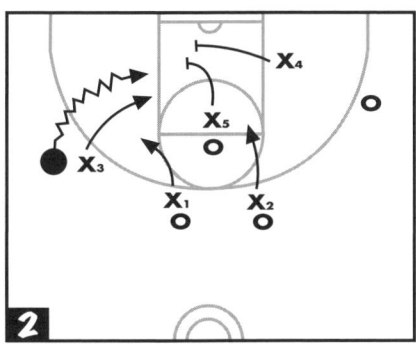

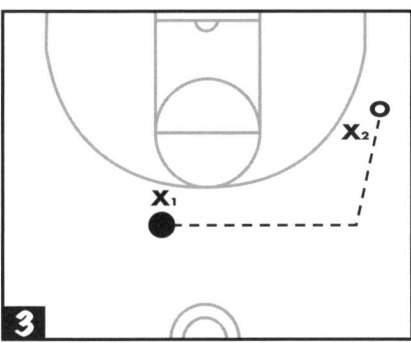

Be "Ball Oriented"

Your players must always be able to see the ball. The ball is the most important thing on the floor. The saying "vision is quickness" is very true, so they need to see the ball and anticipate.

Anticipation

Good defensive players anticipate what the offense is going to do, rather than react after it happens. This is especially true in help and recover situations.

Passing Lane Pressure

Diagram 1 When guarding players without the ball the defender should stay "on the line and up the line".

Once the offensive player moves outside the three-point line, the defender should just be "up the line." Don't allow uncontested shots and don't allow the offense a free look inside.

The "31" Zone Defense
By Thomas J. Moriarty

MY TEAMS HAVE built a reputation using the 1-3-1 extended zone defense ("31"). It has become a trademark of our program and a real sense of pride for our team. The extended 1-3-1 zone is the type of defense that can cause your opponents fits and win a lot of games for your team.

Our "31" zone defense is not a traditional 1-3-1 but an extended zone. In this defense, we pick up the ball at three-quarter-court and pressure it toward the sideline. As the ball approaches midcourt, our wings hedge toward the ball to slow it down, but we do not ever trap the ball. All of our traps are passive traps with the lanes covered. In this defense, you can vary the pickup areas anywhere from the foul line extended out.

WHY AN EXTENDED ZONE ... AND WHEN?

There are a number of good reasons to use an extended zone. For one thing, it forces your opponent to spend valuable time preparing for a defense they don't see often, which takes away from other preparations. Also, most teams have a standard zone or man-to-man offense, but not a standard offense against an extended zone, so most end up in some type of standstill-usually a 2-1-2 set.

Using an extended zone offers us a change of pace defense that can give us a life. (In our case, it also gives us an identity. We take great pride in our extended zone defense, and our players are sold on it). Finally, you can fast-break out of an extended zone very well.

An extended zone defense is effective when used after made baskets or in dead ball situations. Against set-up teams, we can use it against missed or made shots; against some teams we have been able to press and still play an extended zone.

Use this defense early in the game; if it's not effective, you can abandon it and come back to it later. Also, the extended zone is particularly effective if you get ahead; opponents have a tendency to become impatient. Be selective, though. Don't use an extended zone against all teams, or at all times; some teams you have to feel you can beat without a "special" defense. And it's wise to vary your defenses.

POSITIONING, RESPONSIBILITY

We use very few drills in teaching this particular defense. (Two are a ball reaction drill for centers and a shuffle drill.) Rather, we spend a great deal of time explaining positioning, responsibilities and five players working as a unit. We always talk responsibility; it gives our players more freedom.

PLAYER POSITIONING

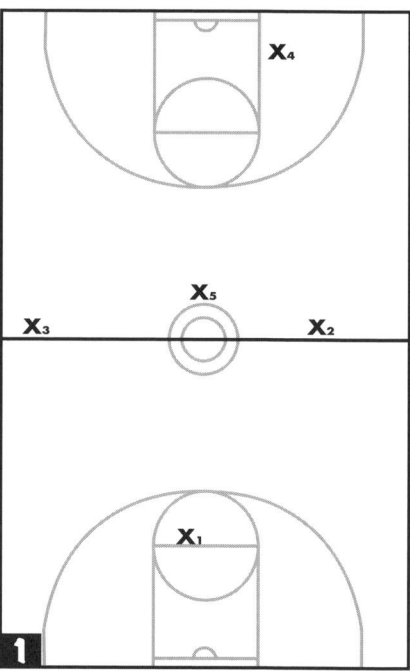

Diagram 1: The initial position of players for this defense. Defender X1 should be your biggest guard — a rebounder who's smart; you must give him or her freedom. Defender X2 should be your quickest forward and X3 your best rebounding forward. Defender X4 is the smallest guard — quick and hard-nosed, to get the charge; the front people must pressure the ball to help.

The ball should be picked up at

three-quarter-court by X1 and forced to one side or the other. X1 should not allow the ball to be brought up the middle of the court.

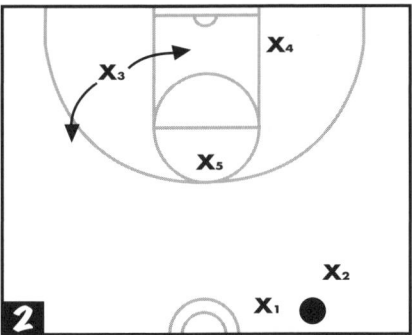

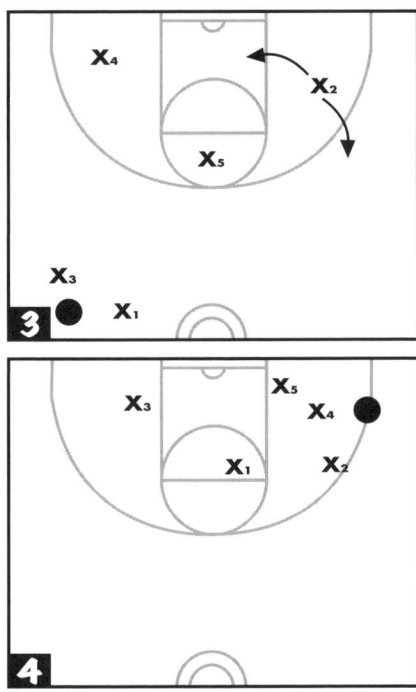

Diagram 2: Ball On Side. With the ball on the right side in the front court, X1 and X2 form a positive trap on the ball, hoping to get a hand on an errant pass or to force the ball to be thrown away (or at least high). Defender X2 is responsible for the entire area to the basket line. Defender X4 remains on the baseline to the ballside of the foul line. X4 must not cheat out, but go when the ball is thrown. Finally, X5 plays the high post man-to-man. If the post player plays low, X5 adjusts accordingly; if there's no post player, the defender simply plays the post area, staying alert for a flashing post.

Diagram 3: If the ball is swung from guard-to-guard (that is side to side) the player responsibilities are the same as just mentioned, only mirrored.

Diagram 4: Ball In Corner. If the ball is swung into the corner, X4 and X2 form a positive trap. Defender X5 moves to the low post area and X1 drops to the foul line. Any player in the high post area is X1's responsibility. Defender X3 moves low, away from the ball.

It's extremely important that all players be aware of the passing lanes and that they try to force the ball to be thrown over the top of the defense. It's also very important that there be constant communication among all players, especially as offensive players move in and out of the post area.

The weak-side forward becomes a quarterback for the defense; that player can see everything when the ball is in the corner.

DEFENSIVE KEYS

To make this defense work, there are several key elements to keep in mind:

1. Do not allow the ball to go to the post area.
2. Your players must not put too much pressure on the ball, but it must look like pressure.
3. Be aware of the passing lanes. Continually force the ball away from the basket.
4. The team must rebound. You should repeatedly go over rebounding assignments; the front player is important.
5. Your players must constantly bounce and change passing lanes. They must also force the ball to be passed over the top of the defense.
6. You must preach to your players to move when the ball is thrown, not when it reaches its target.

There are also a few very important variations to this defense as follows:

32X: Pick up at three-quarter-court and nurse the ball upcourt. It's not a real hard trap; you're simply extending the defense.

Scramble: Out of the "31" trap anywhere, usually around the midcourt area. Called six or eight times a game, it's an excellent change of pace. It's used to pick up the pace of the regular "D" if your players start standing around or getting lazy.

31 hard traps. It's a 1-2-1-1 full-court zone press.

CONCLUSION

With this defense you can control the tempo of the game. It forces opposing teams to take time attacking and makes them alter their offense.

The 1-1-3 Half-Court Trap
By Mike Bartell

THE 1-1-3 HALF court trap is a very aggressive, gambling defense that forces many turnovers which lead to easy baskets.

Initially, it looks very similar to the traditional 1-3-1 half-court trap. However, it has different rules and rotations. Therefore, it will frustrate opposing coaches who attempt to attack the 1-1-3 trap the same way they would attack the 1-3-1 trap.

ADVANTAGES OF THE 1-1-3

1. Force many turnovers which lead to easy fast-break baskets.
2. Create an up-tempo style of play.
3. Show your opponents a different look.
4. Force the opponent out of their normal offense.
5. Force the opponent's best ball handler to give up the basketball.
6. Create defensive excitement for

both the players and the crowd.
7. Most opposing coaches have probably never seen the 1-1-3 trap, thus they won't know how to attack it.
8. It is easily disguised to look like the traditional 1-3-1 trap. However, an effective attack against the 1-3-1 trap becomes ineffective against the 1-1-3.
9. The defense can easily and quickly fall back into a zone (2-3, 2-1-2 or 1-3-1).

feet. A player with some size or long arms would be great to play in this position.

X3 and X4 have to be quick players who can anticipate passes and break on the ball.

X5 should be a good defender who can prevent easy baskets if the trap is broken. This position is good for tall, slower players.

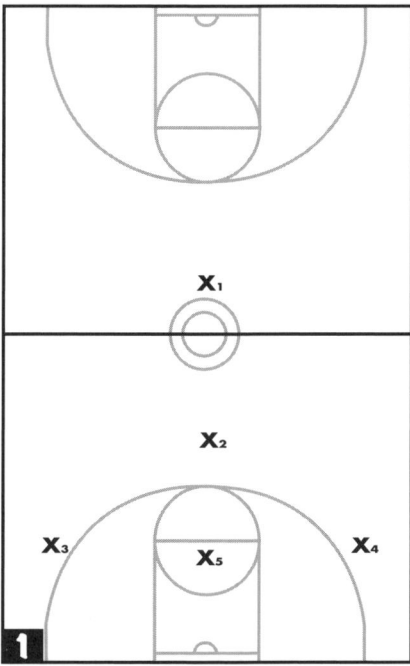

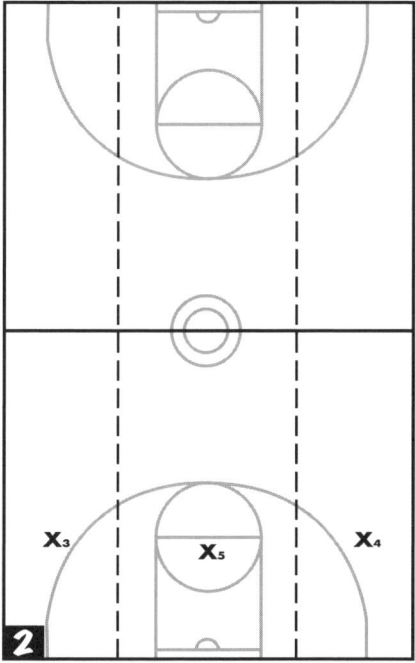

Diagram 1: This is the alignment for the 1-1-3 trap.

X1 is your quickest defensive guard and must be able to shuffle their feet quickly and apply pressure on the ball.

X2 helps trap the dribbler, so they must be able to move their

Diagram 2: X3, X4 and X5 each have their own lane which they are responsible for.

Diagram 3: X1 pressures the ball and forces it to one side. X2 stays in their area until after the ball crosses half court. X3 and X4 start even with the highest player in their respective lane (even in the backcourt) anticipating a pass. They should play slightly off the passing

Half-Court Defense　　　　　　　　　**75**

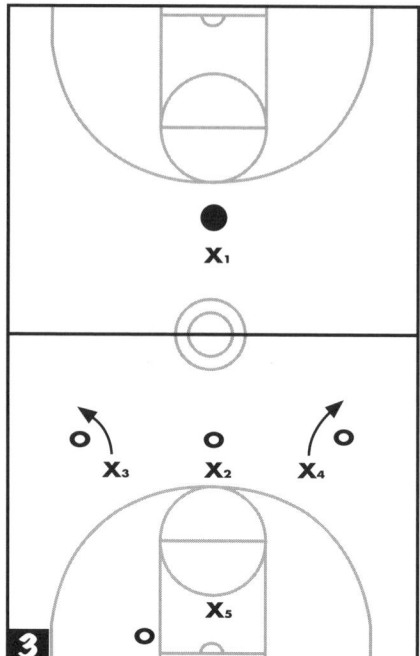
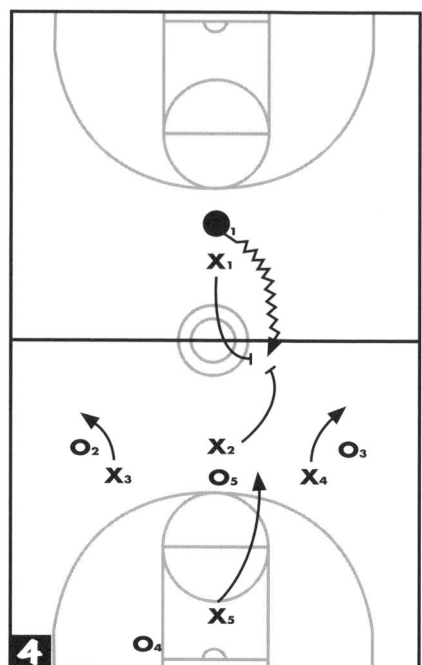

lane in order to make the opposing point guard think the pass is open. X5 protects the basket.

Diagram 4: As soon as the ball crosses half court, X2 comes forward to trap with X1. X2 must cut off the dribbler. Both players must shuffle their feet and work hard to set the trap. X3 and X4 continue to anticipate a pass to the highest offensive player in their lanes (O2 and O3). As the trap on the ball is being set, X5 rotates up to the highest offensive player in their lane (O5). But X5 must be ready to hustle back and protect the basket if the trap is broken.

O4 is left wide open, but if a good trap is set, a pass to O4 is difficult to make. The trapped dribbler (O1) is more likely to look to their primary outlets (O2, O3 or O5) first.

We have a "one and done" trap rule. If the first trap is broken, either by a pass or dribble, we immediately sprint back into a 2-1-2 zone.

ADJUSTING TO THE OFFENSE

Since this defense is unusual, opposing coaches are going to use a variety of different offensive approaches against it. Here are some of those different approaches and how we adjust to defend them.

2-1-2 ATTACK

Diagram 5: The is the offensive setup we defend most often. X4 moves forward to cover O4 (highest player in their lane) to take away the guard-to-guard pass. X1 and X2 trap the offensive point guard. X3 anticipates a pass to O4. X5 rotates up and anticipates a pass to O3.

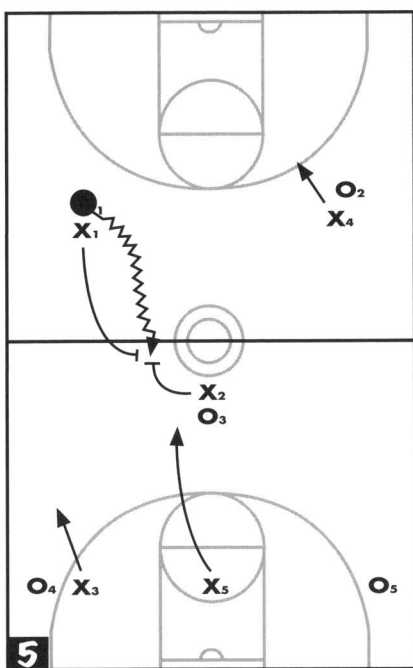

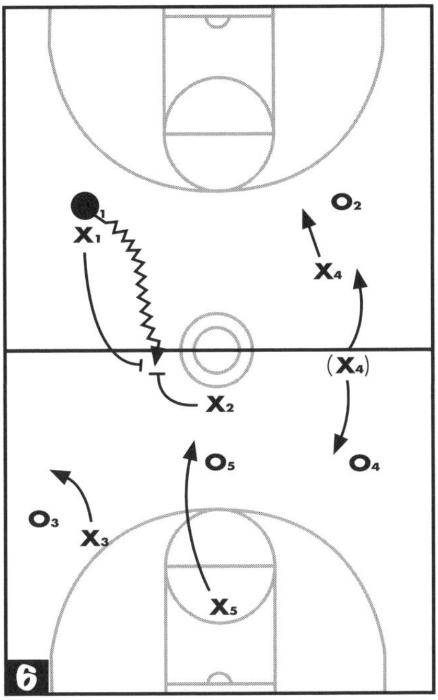

2-3 ATTACK

Diagram 6: This is the most difficult offensive attack to defend. X1 and X2 trap. X3 anticipates the pass to O3. X5 rotates up to anticipate the pass to O5. X4 anticipates the pass to O2, leaving O4 open. If the offense starts to hurt you by passing over the top to O4, X4 might have to drop off and "split the gap" between O2 and O4 and anticipate both passes.

1-2-2 ATTACK

Diagram 7: X1 and X2 trap. X3 and X4 anticipate the pass to the highest player in their lanes. There isn't an offensive player in the high post, so X5 anticipates a pass to one of the players flashing through their lane. If the trap is broken, everyone must hustle back to prevent the easy two-on-one basket.

SECONDARY TRAPS

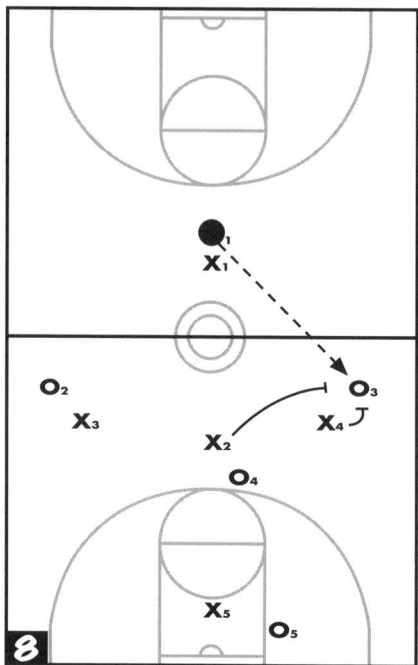

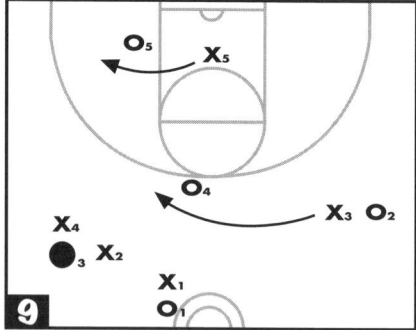

Diagram 8: If a pass to the wing is completed, X2 and the ball-side wing (X4) can trap.

Diagram 9: One way to rotate after the sideline trap is to have X1 stay on the point guard to take away the return pass. X3 rotates to the high-post area. X5 rotates to front the low post.

Diagram 10: The other rotation is to have X1 rotate to the high post.

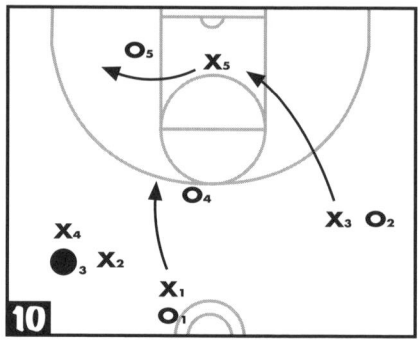

X3 rotates to protect the basket and X5 rotates to front the low post.

GAME ADJUSTMENTS

There are many adjustments to the 1-1-3 half-court trap that you can make during the course of the game.

1. Pick-up point of the basketball can be changed to give additional or less ball pressure.
2. Initiate secondary trapping.
3. X2 can set the trap before the ball crosses half court.
4. X5 can stay behind everyone to protect the basket instead of rotating up.
5. X1 can force the dribbler to a specific direction.
6. X3, X4 and X5 can deny the pass to the highest offensive player in their lanes.
7. Switch in and out of the 1-1-3 and the 1-3-1 trap defenses to change the trapping schemes throughout the game.

The 1-1-3 half-court trap has been extremely effective for us. It has simple rules and responsibilities for each position and is easy to teach. It will force countless turnovers and produce easy baskets.

2-1-2 Half-Court Trapping Defense
By John Ford

THE 2-1-2 HALF-COURT trapping defense causes havoc against the opposition. You'll find this defense is effective because many offenses do not see a 2-1-2 extended to half court.

Don't use this defense for extended time periods or it loses effectiveness. Try not to use it in more than two consecutive possessions or out of dead-ball situations.

Use the defense as an element of surprise to throw your opponent's offense out of sync. This is a good defense to surprise an opponent that knows your team well.

Encourage the offense to make skip passes or diagonal passes. Prepare your defenders to key on certain designated passing lanes and play for the steal.

Designate areas where "sucker passes" are supposed to go. Send your second defender to trap the ball in those areas.

Have your defense anticipate and react to where the passes are going. Prepare your players to attack "trap" and "steal" areas to force turnovers and get steals.

The advantages of the scheme are:
✔ It causes problems by shocking the offense.
✔ It gives your opponent more to prepare for when playing your team.
✔ It can be used with a small, quick team or a slow, tall team.
✔ It keeps the opposing offense from getting into rhythm.
✔ It forces the offense to set up farther away from the basket.
✔ It forces steals and leads to easy fast-break scoring opportunities.

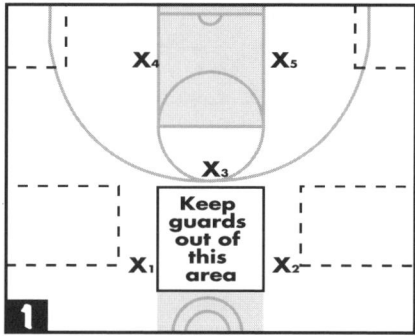

Diagram 1: The dotted areas are for traps. Shaded areas can be defended by one player using the sideline and half-court line for help.

X3 is your best and quickest defender who preferably has good size. X1 and X2 must keep the ball out of the middle. X1 and X2 can be small, but must be able to drive the ball to the wing or force a pass to the wing. You can go "big" and force your opponent to pass over the top.

X4 and X5 can be post or perimeter players depending on your needs at the top of the defense.

Force the defense to pass into the designated trap areas, where your players should force the steal. Your defense must be able to read the coming pass while it is in the air, react and shift accordingly. Shaded areas are where the defense must defend or steal after your players trap on the wing.

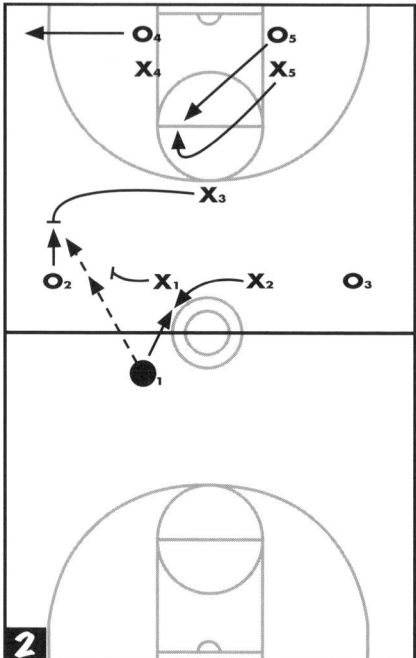

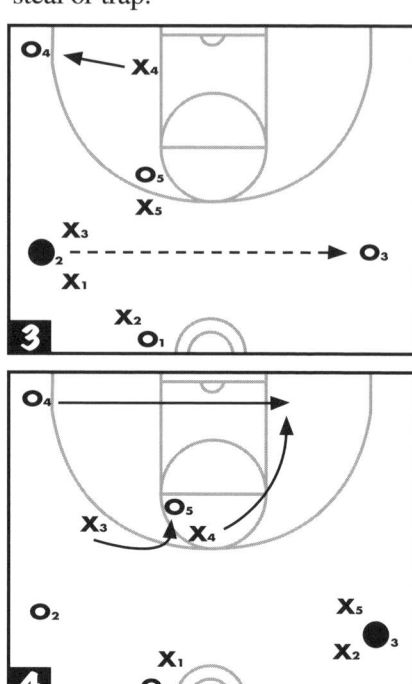

Diagram 2: If none of your players set at the high post, O4 or O5 will flash to the spot. X5 must match up in that area.

X2 denies the return pass to O1, allowing O2 to pass to O4 in the corner. The corner pass is ideal for the next trap. The other option is a skip pass to O3. If the skip pass is attempted, X2 and X5 should read and react for a steal.

Diagram 3: Count on X3 and X1 to block the vision of the skip pass to O3, leaving the pass to O3. X2 and X5 should react to the pass to O3 while it is in the air to set up a steal or trap.

Diagram 4: X5 and X2 trap. X4 fronts O5. X3 splits O2 and O4. X1 denies O1 from 3-point line and beyond.

Key: If O4 goes to the ball side, X3 and X4 defend with X4 dropping to cover O4 and X3 replacing X4's position. This allows the long, easily intercepted pass to O2.

Diagram 5: If O3 flashes to the ball side, X5 is in good position to split O5 and O3. If O3 flashes a little higher, X2 can split the two.

Diagram 6: The offense will try to get the ball in the middle. Your defense must anticipate, wait for the pass and go for the steal (hence the name "sucker pass").

The only passes O2 can make

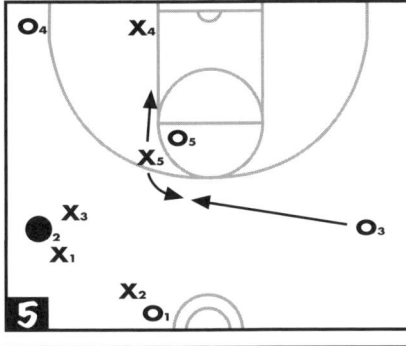

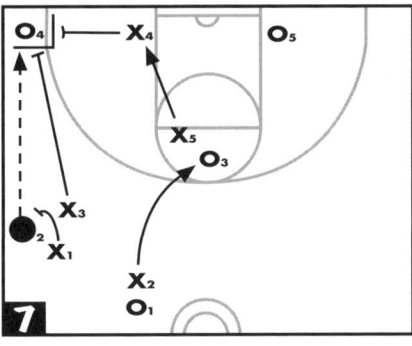

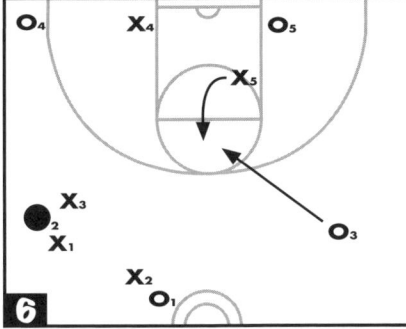

are to O4 or O5. You want the pass to go to O4 to set up the second trap. The diagonal pass to O5 sets up an easy steal.

Diagram 7: On the second pass to O4, the defense makes these shifts:
✔ X4 and X3 trap in the corner.
✔ X1 denies O2 or splits O2 and O1 if O1 comes to the ball side.
✔ X5 drops to the ball-side block.
✔ X2 drops to the high post.

Key: Your trappers must run into trap positions with their hands up to make seeing the passing lanes difficult for the offense.

Diagram 8: This is what your shift looks like. The shift only allows the long pass to O1. X1 and X2 should read the pass and steal the ball. If O1 flashes to the ball, X1 splits O1 and O2 or denies O1.

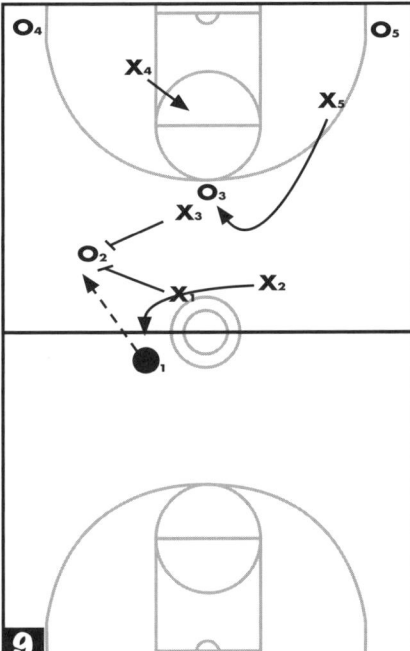

Diagram 9: If the offense posts a player or tries to spread the

Half-Court Defense

defense, defend the play as follows:
- ✔ X1 and X3 trap while X2 denies O1.
- ✔ X5 defends O3 and X4 splits O4 and O5 by stepping up in the key.

Note: O2 has two options: a cross-court pass to O5 that X4 should steal or a safer pass to O4 that X4 and X3 can double-team.

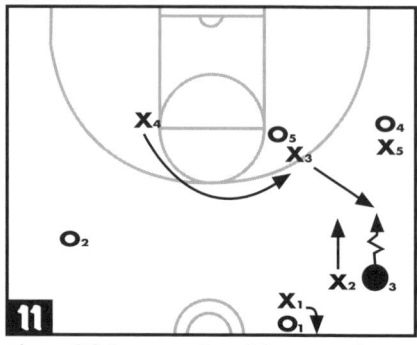

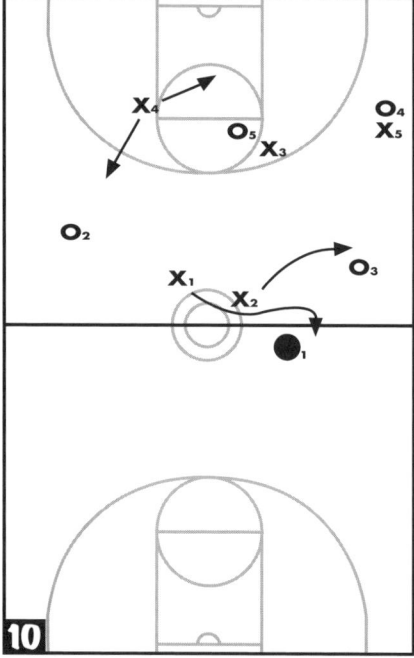

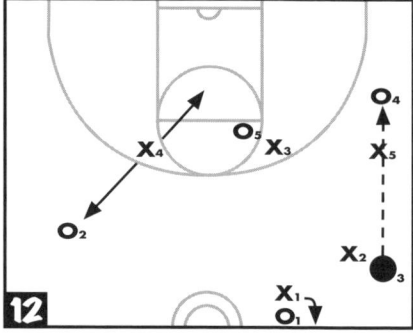

tion. O2 is open, but it's a tough pass for the offense to make in front of two defenders.

Diagram 10: You want the offense to overload one side or move its players higher. O3 is not in a trap area so X2 can defend O3. X1 denies O1. X5 matches up with O4. X3 fronts O5. X4 splits responsibility of defending O2 and the key and is ready for a pass to O2 from O3.

Diagram 11: The rotation follows with X3 and X2 trapping and X4 replacing X3 at the high-post posi-

Diagram 12: If O3 makes the pass to O4, X5 forces O4 to the baseline so that X3 can trap.

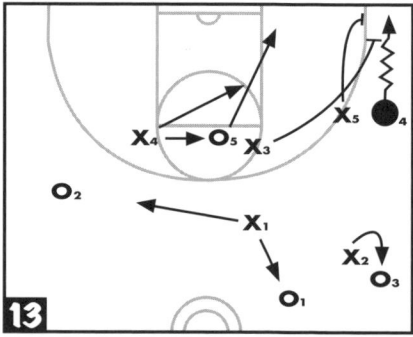

Diagram 13: X3 and X5 trap O4. O5 usually drops to the ball-side block near X4's defensive responsibility. If O5 keeps high-post position, X4 defends. X2 denies O3. X1

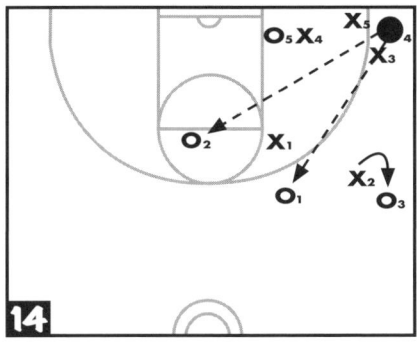

splits O1 and O2 and prepares to steal. X1 knows a pass may come.
Diagram 14: O4's passing options are difficult out of the trap. Both passes should be stolen and turned into a scoring opportunity.

You'll find this defense creates problems for the opposition if it is used infrequently.

2-2-1 Half-Court Press
By Buster Harvey

BYPRODUCTS OF PRESS: WHY?
✔ Exciting style of play.
✔ It gets your players in good condition.
✔ Creates tempo.
✔ Players and fans love it.

GOALS: WHAT WE WANT?
✔ Offset the pace of opponents.
✔ To show a different look in a half-court press set.
✔ Set tempo of game.
✔ Force mistakes. Force errors — get them to rush their offense, upset their offensive flow, force time-outs, etc.
✔ Apply constant pressure.
✔ Players are conditioned to play hard for the entire game.

EXECUTION, KEY NOTES
Diagram 1: Formation.
✔ Use after a score, free throw (made or missed), dead ball or missed shot.

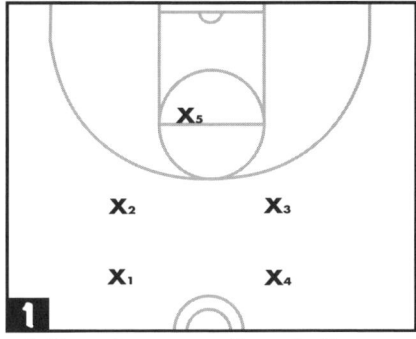

✔ Trapping areas: force ball toward sidelines and trap the ball wherever it goes.
✔ Continue to trap ball, no matter where it goes.
✔ Apply constant pressure and it will create mistakes.

RULES
✔ Force the ball toward sidelines and trap.
✔ Coverage: side, middle, basket (must turn sideways).
✔ Utilize good trapping techniques (L trap).

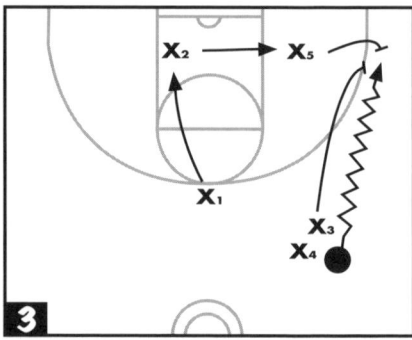

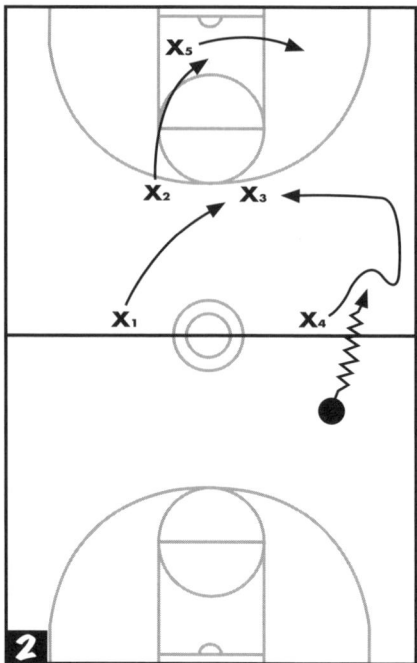

- ✔ Hands should apply constant pressure. Use them to try to influence these offensive variables:
  1. How they pass.
  2. Where they pass.
- ✔ Keep the ball out of middle. Explain to your players what happens when ball goes to middle.
- ✔ Don't foul.

OTHER NOTES
- ✔ Your defenders must attack the ball and try to force to an area where a trap can be successful.
- ✔ Trap the ball wherever it's passed. Continue to trap the ball on every pass.

- ✔ Stress to your players that they cannot allow anyone to dribble by them.
- ✔ Move quick and be active.

COVERAGE AND ROTATIONS
Diagrams 2, 3:
- ✔ Always cover the side and middle basket areas.
- ✔ Reverse rotation if ball goes to opposite side.
- ✔ If there's a breakdown, all players should retreat to the paint and try to force the ball back outside and continue to trap.

POSITIONS
- ✔ Remember that every team you play will be different. What worked good against one opponent, may not work against others.
- ✔ Fit the positioning of your defense to fit your personnel.
- ✔ Go over your system with your players every day in practice.

Chapter 5

Set Defense

1-3-1 Passing Lane Defense
By Jack Thigpen

THIS DEFENSE IS different from the standard 1-3-1 zone. We spread the defense over the entire half court area and play in all of the passing lanes. Our objective is to make the offense go over the top of a defensive player for every pass.

If properly played, the opponent's offense will be forced out higher and wider than normal when attacking this defense. It should also confuse the offense and usually results in several easy turnovers as well as a long time to adjust their offensive attack.

I have used this defense very successfully in high school and have seen it used as effectively on the college level. It's especially tough in small gyms where the area to cover is not as large.

Size of the defensive players is not essential. The most important factor is for the players to react quickly to the ball and realize that they must move and not stand still. All five defenders must move on each pass.

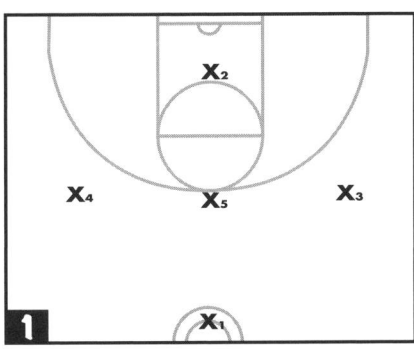

Diagram 1: The basic alignment.

PLAYER RESPONSIBILITIES

Here are the responsibilities for each defender in the 1-3-1 passing lane defense.

Point (X1)
1. Set up at half court or higher.
2. Force the ball handler to go to one side or the other. Do not let

Set Defense 85

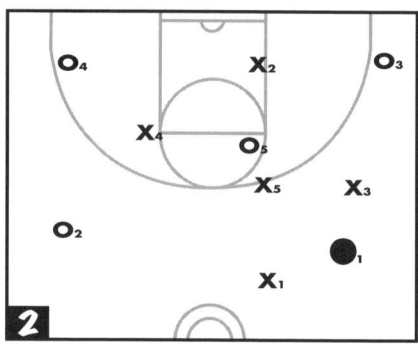
Diagram 2: The defense with the ball at the guard.

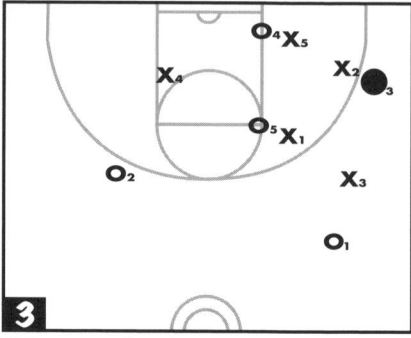
Diagram 3: The defense with the ball in the corner.

the offense dribble from one side to the other.
3. If the ball is on one side but above the wings, stay high and prevent a cross-court reversal pass.
4. If the ball is passed to the corner, 1 must drop to the high post area and front any player there.

Wings (X3-X4)
1. Set up high and wide — top of circle extended. Face the guard with your back to the offensive forward and play in the passing lane between the guard and forward.
2. Don't let the dribbler penetrate any higher than the top of the circle. Don't let the offense dribble down the sideline.
3. If the ball is thrown to the corner, turn and face the ball. Don't let the ball be passed back to the guard on your side.
4. If the ball is on the opposite side, drop in the lane area and cover any offensive player in the low post area.
5. If the ball is passed from the opposite corner across to the

guard on your side, move quickly up high and wide and keep the ball at the guard position.

Center (X5)
1. Start at the top of the circle fronting the offensive center.
2. Stop guard penetration if they try to drive down the middle.
3. If the ball is passed to the corner, immediately drop to the low post fronting the low offensive center.

Back Defender (X2)
1. Start in the lane at the broken line. Watch for the lob pass to the center from the guard. Front any low post offensive player.
2. Always have at least one foot in the lane until the ball goes to the corner.
3. If the ball goes to the corner, immediately move out and guard the player with the ball. Be sure not to let the offensive player drive the baseline.
4. When the ball leaves the corner, immediately move back to the low post with at least one foot in the lane.

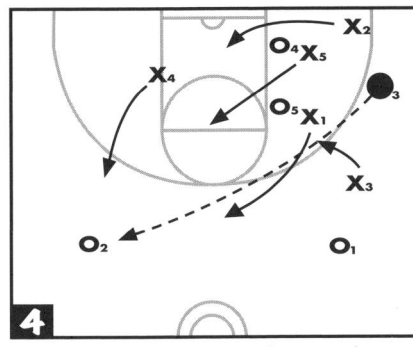

Diagram 4: Here are the rotations on the skip pass out of the corner.

5. It's the responsibility of the back defender to talk and direct the defense. He or she should talk and help the center who is fronting the offensive center. They should also help the wings as they face the ball and have their back to the offensive players.

Remember, this is a passing lane defense. Make the offense throw the lob pass, then react as soon as the ball is thrown with all five players moving quickly.

By playing this defense, you can force the offense out wide and away from the basket.

The 3-2 Distorted Zone Defense
By Jack Fertig

MOST ZONE DEFENSES are symmetrical, that is, the coverages on one side of the floor are the same as the coverages on the other side. Maybe that's the reason zone offenses are also symmetrical-movements to one side are the same as movements to the other. Today's players are getting so good and are so instinctive, wouldn't it be to the defense's advantage to show a different look in order to confuse the offense?

The 3-2 defense has been used in many different ways. One of the methods is the "point-drop," which offers the following coverage:

When the ball is passed from the wing to the corner, the bottom defender plays the ball and the point defender drops to guard the low post (Diagram 1). There are a couple of drawbacks to this type of coverage: One, you really wear out X3, and two, you have a near impossible coverage (from fronting one low post to fronting the other) when a corner-to-corner skip pass is made (Diagram 2). In addition, your big players (X4 and X5) have to guard

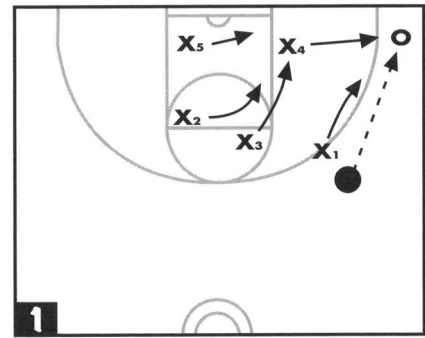

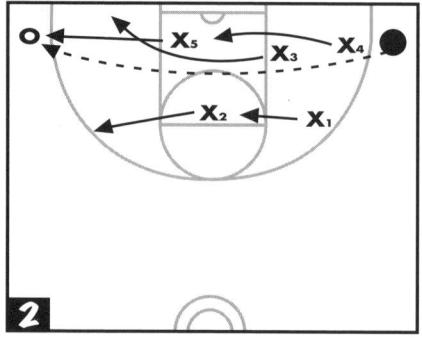

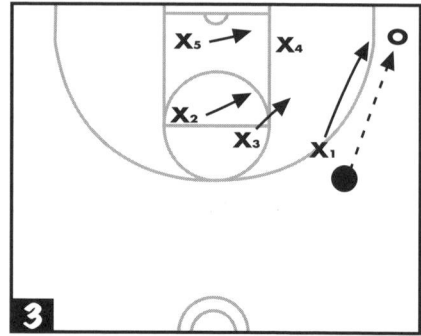

the corner, which takes them away from rebounding position.

Should you want to keep your rebounders inside, you may have your wings (X1 and X2) cover wing-to-corner passes (Diagram 3). The problem is that you wear out your wing players as well, especially against teams that pass wing-to-corner and back repeatedly.

The solution could be to combine the two coverages using the strengths of each and more or less eliminating the weaknesses.

First, it's necessary to look at your personnel. Your two back defenders will probably be your 4 and 5 players (power forward and center). The better rebounder of the two should play on the left side (as you look at the basket). The point needs to be your best athlete but should have some size, so it will probably be your small forward, or 3 player. This leaves players 1 and 2 (point and shooting guards) to play the wings. Whichever of these two is the deeper position for you should play the right wing. Assuming you have a good point guard and an average backup point, plus

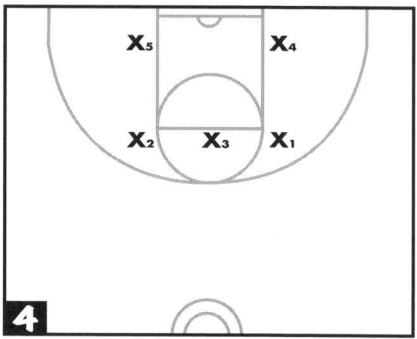

three good — or at least equal — second guards, and assuming your center (5) is your best rebounder, your defensive alignment is as shown in Diagram 4.

Your coverages when the ball is on the right side and when it's on the left side are shown in diagrams 5 and 6, respectively. There are three distinct advantages to this distorted alignment:

1. X5, your best rebounder, stays inside and is always rebounding.
2. X3 has to play only from the free-throw line to the right block (as opposed to the triangle, right block, free-throw line and left block, as in the point-drop).
3. The player you're asking to work hardest is X2, where you are deepest and can substitute.

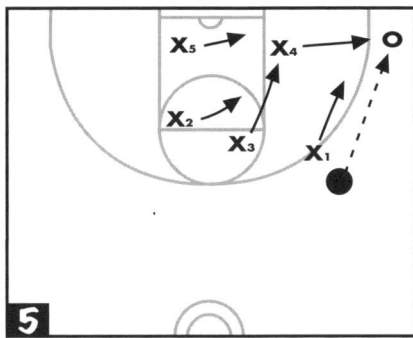 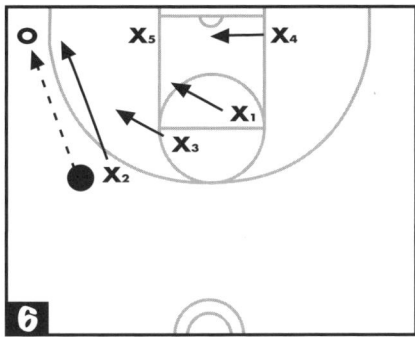

In addition, since most teams are right-hand oriented, most shots will come from the right side; therefore, most rebounds will come to the left side, where X5, your best rebounder, is stationed.

If an offense is symmetrical, this defense will give it different, confusing looks. For example, if the ball goes to the left corner, your wing plays it; if it goes to the right corner, your baseline defender plays it.

Teams that like to screen will have problems with this defense because who they need to screen on one side isn't who should be screened on the other.

This distorted 3-2 look may give you the psychological edge you need while still allowing you to use a fundamentally sound defense.

Playing Man-To-Man Pressure Defense
By Mark Comstock

OUR DEFENSIVE PHILOSOPHY is to force our opponents to change their style of play under game conditions and to do things they don't work on in practice. Taking away passing lanes, forcing errors and disrupting an opponent's offensive patterns are just a few things you can do by being the aggressor on defense. This philosophy makes us not only a strong defensive team, but a consistent team, as well. We believe that our defense will keep us in any ballgame regardless of our point production.

Changing defenses is also an important part of our defensive philosophy. We feel that our man-to-man pressure is our main defense, and all our other defenses build out from it. Many other ingredients determine where we pick up our opponents — full-court, three-quarters or half-court.

We use three principles in teaching man-to-man pressure:
1. Put intelligent pressure on the ball at all times.
2. Use extreme denial one pass

away (including guard-to-guard) and to any post player (high or low).
3. Always have a defender from the weak side ready to help cover up penetration. Along with those three principles, we use other defensive tactics to pressure our opponents, among them diving, hedging, jump-switching, blitz-switching, run-and-jump trapping and rotating.

PRESSURE ON THE BALL

You must instill in your players the need to have pressure on the ball. If you allow guards room to work, they'll pick you apart with penetration and passing. If you can keep good pressure on the ball at all times, you've taken a big step in the right direction of sound man-to-man pressure defense. This also makes everyone else's job easier, and they become more effective players.

The main points of emphasis for putting pressure on the ball are as follows:
1. Maintain intelligent pressure on the ball — don't foul.
2. Always stay belly-up with your opponents.
3. Discourage penetration!
4. Force the offensive player to pick up the dribble, then jump or close; yell, "Cover!"
5. Force to the outside.

DENIAL ONE PASS AWAY

All five defensive players must be ready to deny their opponents. The most important rule in denial is to see both the ball and the opponents at all times. We don't want our players opening up to the ball. Players deny their opponent by being belly-up when the opponent cuts behind — staying belly-up and snapping the head to find the ball. We deny guard-to-guard passes, which puts added pressure on the opposing guards.

Many coaches might argue against this idea, but is has been very successful for us. Aggressive denial forces opponents into errors by disrupting their timing and patterns.

The main points of emphasis for denial one pass away are as follows:
1. Use extreme denial one pass away.
2. Force the opponent backdoor.
3. Keep your body and ball-side hand in the passing lane.
4. See the ball and the opponent.
5. Belly-up defense applies. We never allow our players to open up to the ball. We deny belly-up and snap the head to find the ball.
6. Deny any opponent posting up high or low.
7. Force lob passes.
8. Be ready for X-ing (see below).
9. Be ready to defend two-player plays.

HELP FROM THE WEAK SIDE

In order to play pressure defense, you must have consistent weak-side help or your team will not be as aggressive as it could be. Players must feel that if their assigned opponent gets behind them or penetrates, they'll still not get scored upon. The weak-side defenders must also be aware of their own assigned opponent so if the player flashes, that person doesn't give the offense an easy outlet. The weak-side defender must be ready and in position to help and deny; that player is the catalyst in successful man-to-man defense.

The main points of emphasis for help from the weak-side are as follows:

1. Always be in help position if your assigned opponent is two passes away from the ball.
2. See both the ball and the assigned opponent at all times.
3. Be in either Help 1 or Help 2 position.
4. Be ready to deny if your assigned opponent flashes.
5. Be ready for X-ing.
6. Meet guard penetration at the free-throw line.
7. Meet forward penetration two to three steps outside the lane area.
8. Draw the charge.

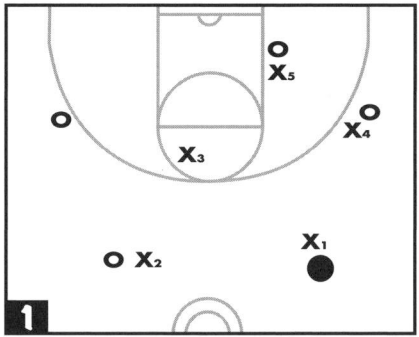

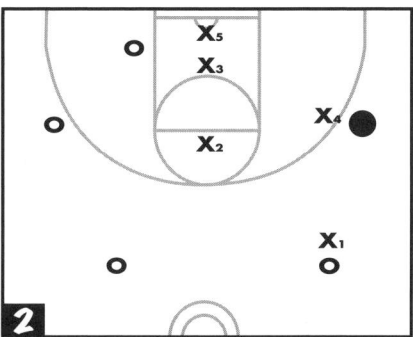

Diagrams 1 through 7 illustrate the player assignments in our pressure defense scheme. Diagram 1 shows how we line up with the ball at the guard position. Notice that the opposite defensive guard is in denial position. Diagram 2 shows how we play when the ball gets into the defensive forward position. We always have our weak-side help defenders in a Help 1 or Help 2 position, so that if they have to stop penetration, they'll meet the offensive player outside the lane area. We always deny the ball into a flashing post, an opponent posting up or a roll player. Anytime the ball gets into the lane through a pass or dribble, we feel our opponent has penetrated our defense. All five defenders dive to the lane area and force the ball back out, then recover to their original assigned opponents or find an open player.

Whenever we get penetration from the guard or forward position, we use a technique called X-ing and Rotation. This technique must be drilled every day to ensure consistent results. Diagram 3 shows an example of baseline penetration. If

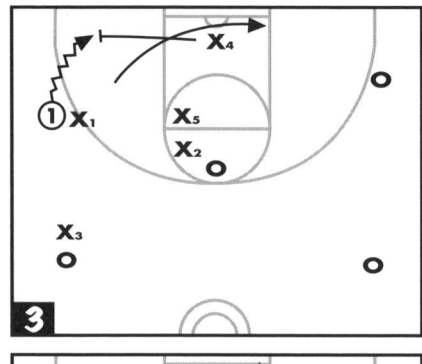

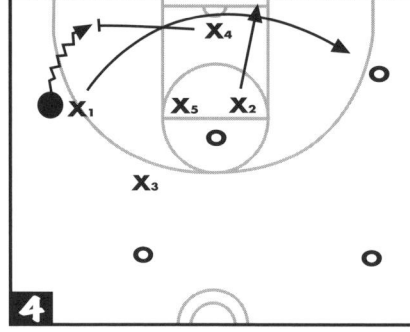

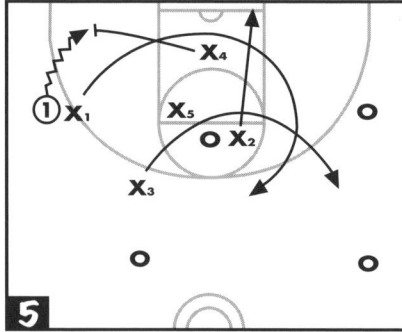

defensive player X1 gets penetrated baseline, then weak-side help defender X4 and X with X1. Double X-ing takes place when X2 beats X1 to cover X4's originally assigned opponent; in that case, X1 continues up to find a player — probably X2's player (Diagram 4). This is called Double X-ing with Rotation. Triple X-ing may take place (Diagram 5) if X3 goes over to pick up X2's assigned opponent.

We never allow our player defending the high post area to get involved in the X-ing and Rotation.

We never switch off the ball and always jump-switch on lateral crossing guards. These techniques must be drilled every day so there's no confusion out on the floor. Communication is extremely important to a successful pressure defense. Always have the defender not guarding the ball calling, "Switch!" or "Stay!" Teach your players not to get picked. We've found that the best technique is for the player to get super tight to the assigned player just before the pick is set so that the defender can beat the pick by going over the top of it. The defensive player guarding the picker must hedge, talk and be ready to switch.

Another technique that must be followed is that the strong-side forward (X1) not come off their assigned player to help on guard dribble penetration. This means that the weak-side forward (X4) must come to help and X with the defender guarding the ball (Diagram 6). The strong-side forward must stay with the assigned opponent and deny so the guard doesn't kick the ball back out for a short, uncontested jumper, as shown in Diagram 7. The weak-side help must come early or it will be wasted. We like to see our help on guard penetration be at the free-throw line and on forward penetration be two

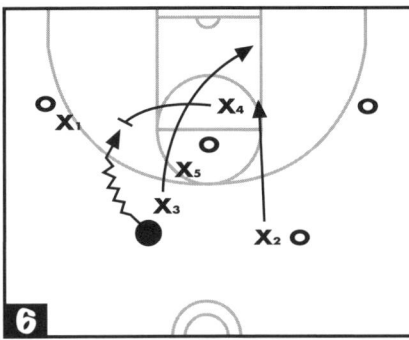
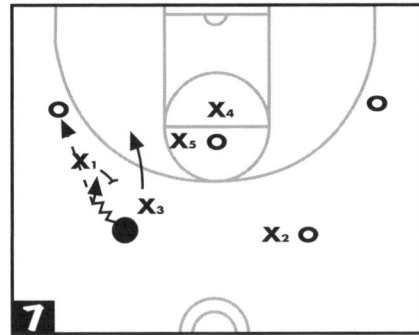

to three steps outside the lane area, with the weak-side help defender coming in both situations.

We believe that pressure defense is the best way to achieve success. Due to this philosophy, we spend a tremendous amount of practice time drilling defense.

Try Man-To-Man Thumbs Down Defense
By Mark Porter

EVERY PROGRAM I'VE been part of has been built on man-to-man defense. We feel it's better to do one or two things very well, rather than five or six things just average.

When the kids in our program were not as quick as others, we made adjustments in our man-to-man defense. The result was sagging man-to-man which we call "thumbs down" ("thumbs up" is our regular denial).

While we've used this "thumbs down" defense in the past against a great penetrator and good post player, it really helps your kids compete when they are overmatched in terms of quickness.

The defense is based on the position of the ball and a 15 foot square box that we have marked on the floor at every practice. We give our players rules to follow so they know exactly where they should be at all times.

We want pressure on the basketball at all times. But when your player's opponent does not have the ball, we want our defensive players to keep at least one foot in the box so we are in a much better position to help and recover.

BALL-SIDE AND HELP-SIDE PRIORITIES

Diagram 1: Defensive Areas.

Ball Side: This is the side of the floor that the ball is on.

✔ **Pressure On The Ball:** Anytime an assigned opponent has the ball we want that player pressured so tightly, that they cannot pass, dribble or shoot the ball easily.

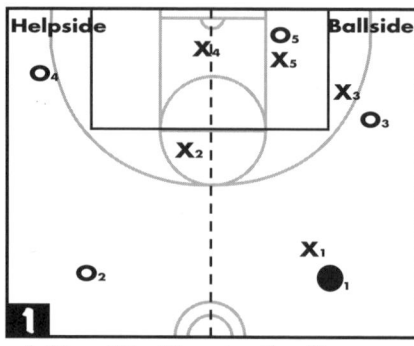

✔ **Stop The Penetrating Pass:** Anytime the ball is passed into our box, we want ball-you-man positioning. We want to stop any penetrating pass into the box. On the perimeter of the box, we want players to recognize situations and anticipate a pass to steal. When our assigned opponent receives the ball on the perimeter, it's important that we closeout with the proper footwork and hand placement while pressuring the ball.

✔ **Stop The Penetrating Move:** Players must position themselves in the box according to the position of the ball, their opponent and the rules of the box. Stopping dribble penetration is a top priority of our defense.

✔ **Double Down On The Post:** Anytime the ball is passed into the post, double team and force the post player to pass the ball out.

✔ **Stop The Ball Reversal:** Recognizing situations and anticipating bad passes comes into play here.

Help Side: This refers to the side of the floor away from the ball. This is what we want from side help:

✔ Players should be in position to help a ball-side defender if beaten.

✔ They should stop penetrating pass and drives.

✔ Players need to stop penetrating cuts to the ball.

These help-side rules are used by players situated both inside and outside the box.

GENERAL RULES

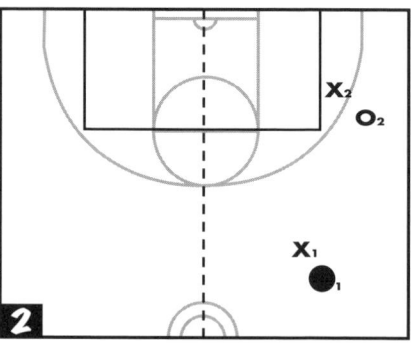

Diagram 2: Perimeter Spacing.

✔ **Ball-You-Man** (Triangle with the box): If a player's opponent does not have the ball, they should stay in a triangle with the assigned opponent and the ball in line with the zone line with one foot in the box.

✔ **As The Ball Moves, You Move:** This is essential to maintain solid team defense. A common phrase that can be used in teaching this is to "jump to the ball."

PLACEMENT RULES FOR THE HELP SIDE

Diagram 3: Players must defend their opponent above the foul line.

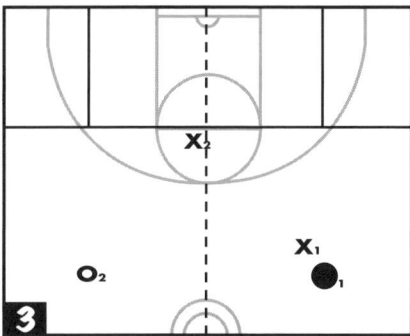

Players should maintain a position on the zone line with one foot in the box.

Defending Assigned Opponent Below The Foul Line:

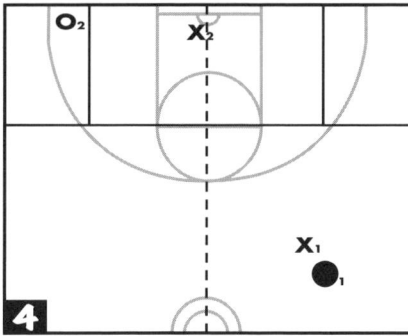

Diagram 4: When the ball is above the foul line. Players should maintain a position near the A zone line. Both feet should be in the lane and player B should be able to see both the assigned opponent and the ball while remaining in a closed position to the ball.

Diagram 5: When the ball is below the foul line, players should maintain a position on the A zone line slightly open to the ball, but still able to see both the opponent and the ball.

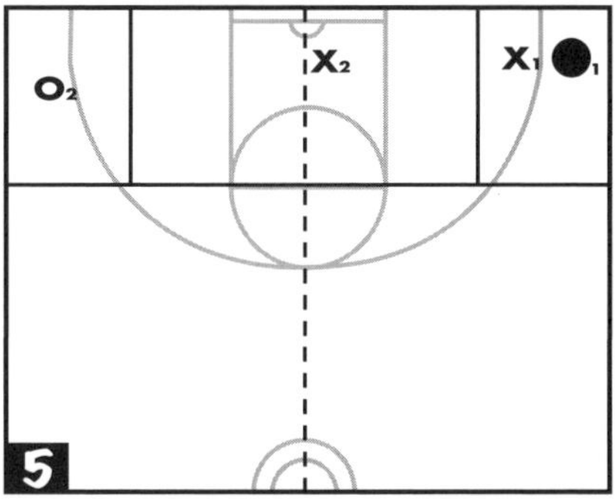

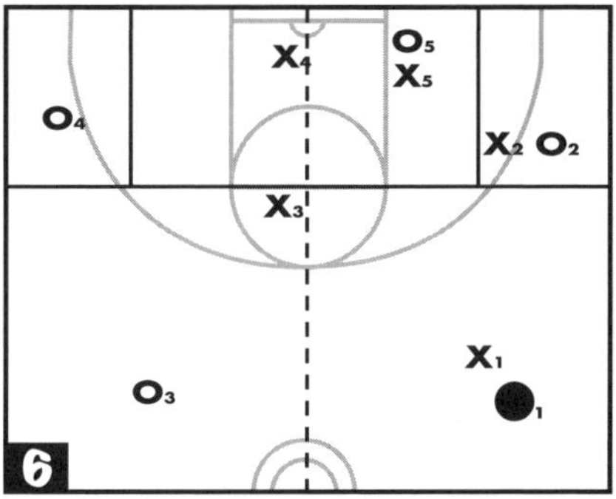

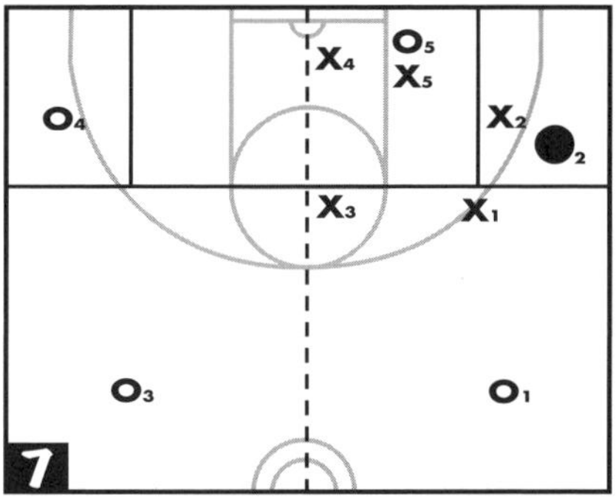

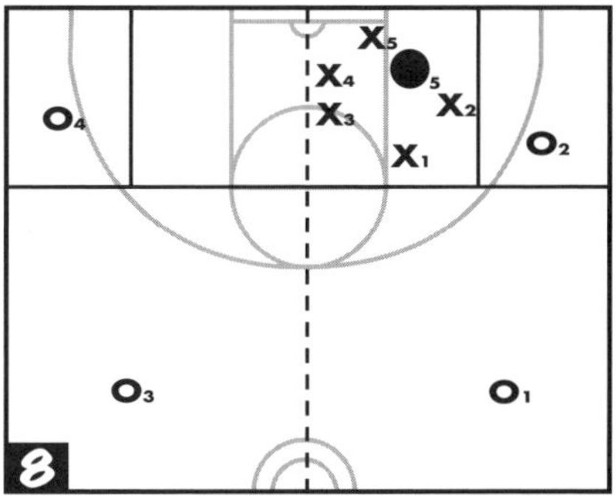

Set Defense 95

BALL SIDE AND HELP SIDE COMBINED

Diagrams 6, 7 & 8: All players are following our basic rules and priorities. They all see the ball and are ready to move as the ball moves.

- ✔ **As The Ball Moves, We Move:** Have pressure on the ball and all defensive players are in a good help position.
- ✔ **As The Ball Moves Into The Post**: Double down and force 5 to kick the ball back out.

Mixing Up Your 1-2-2 Zone
By Scott Barnett

CHANGING YOUR DEFENSES during the course of a game can be very effective. I have found a 1-2-2 zone can be modified on the fly by making calls from the bench. It can also be adjusted to fit your personnel.

The first step is to learn the basic rules of a 1-2-2 zone that we call "12 Stay." From there you can change the defense over the course of the year to have the full package in by season's end.

12 STAY

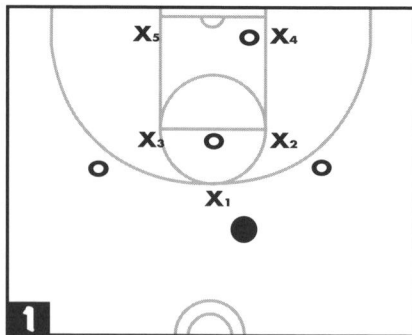

Diagram 1: This is the basic 1-2-2 (12 Stay) set. X1 is usually your smallest, quickest guard responsible for getting the ball out of the middle. X1 has ball responsibility whenever the ball is above the foul line. X2 and X3 must stop any gap drives. X4 and X5 will stay on the blocks.

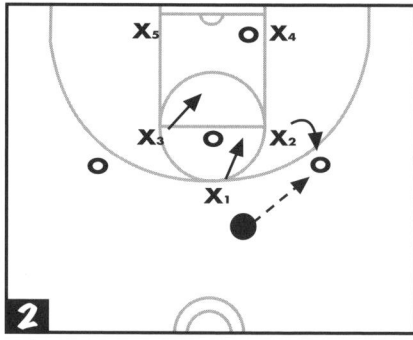

Diagram 2: When the ball is passed to the wing, X1 sinks to cover the high post. X2 and X3 have ball responsibility. If the ball is on the opposite wing, they must sink to the middle and help with the high post. X4 and X5 must front ball-side post. When away from the ball, they must sink to the middle to stop any lobs.

Diagram 3: If the ball goes to the corner, X2 and X3 must follow the ball. X4 and X5 must stop any baseline drives.

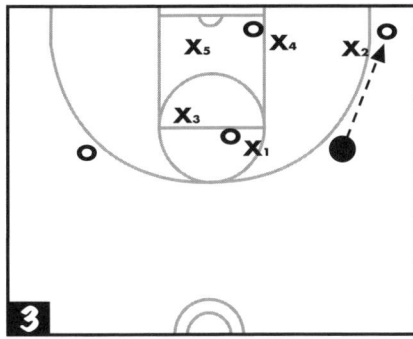

12 GO

12 Go is good against a team with good outside shooters, especially in the corners. It helps if X2 and X3 are tall, because they will be responsible for fronting the post. It is also important for X4 and X5 to be very aggressive on the ball to stop entry passes to the post.

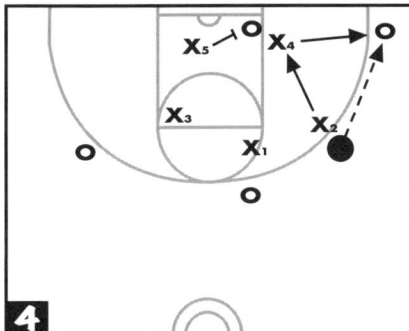

Diagram 4: When the ball is passed to the corner, X4 and X5 will step out to cover it being very aggressive to stop the entry pass. If not on the ball side, they must help the ball side until the wing gets there. X2 and X3 will dive to the ball-side post and front the block. X1 has the same responsibilities as in 12 stay.

Diagram 5: When the ball is reversed back to the wing, X2 and

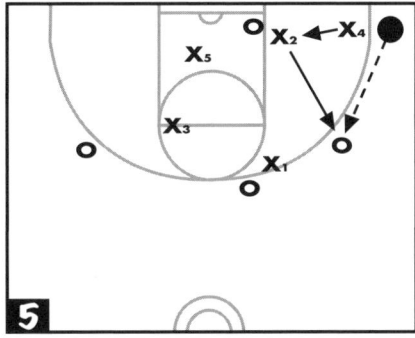

X3 must hustle back to the wing. X4 and X5 return to front the block.

12 TRAP

12 Trap is an excellent half court or three-quarter court trap. The idea is to trap the ball along the sideline and force turnovers. Stress to your players that most steals come from the player in the passing lane, not the ones doing the trapping.

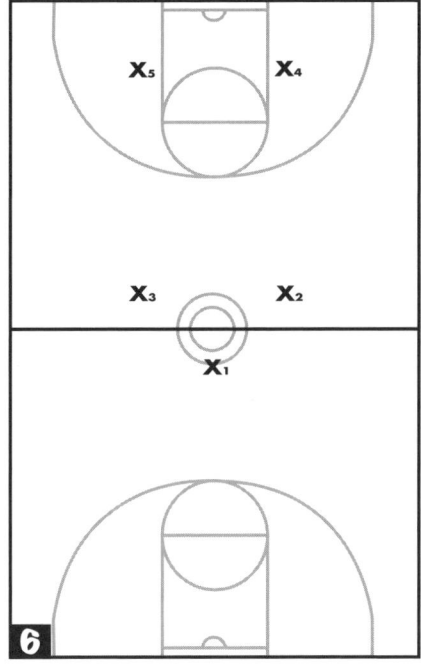

Diagram 6: This is the basic set.

Set Defense

X1 picks up the ball at three-quarter court or half court and tries to force the ball to one side. Get on the side of the ball handler but do not allow a split.

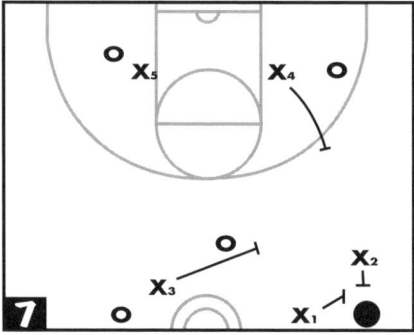

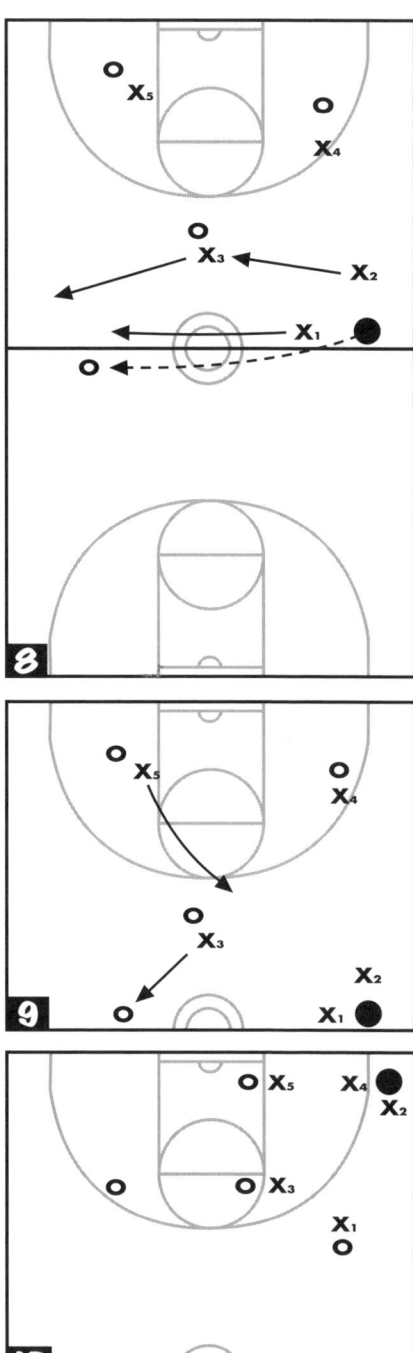

Diagram 7: X2 and X3 must trap at the side line and can not allow the ball to split them and X1. If the ball is away, they must cover the middle and deny at all costs. X4 and X5 to the ball side must be ready to come up and steal a long pass. Off side must protect the basket.

Diagram 8: On a reversal pass, X1 must sprint to the ball and force it into a trap. X2 and X3 do not leave the middle until the opposite guard bumps them from the responsibility.

Diagram 9: If X1 and X2 (or X3 if on the left) have a good sideline trap, X3 can leave the middle to steal the reversal pass. If X3 leaves, then X5 will run to the middle looking for a steal.

12 CORNER

12 Corner can be run as its own defense or as something to fall back into after the offense breaks the 12 Trap. It runs the same as 12 Go until the ball goes into the corner.

Diagram 10: When the ball goes

into the corner, X2 will follow the ball into the corner to set up a trap with X4. X1 rotates to face guard to the ball side to deny the ball reversal. X3 steps over to deny the high post if an opponent is there; if not, look to steal the lob. X5 moves around to front the ball side post. This is where a majority of your steals will come from.

Man-To-Man Pressure Defense Revisited
By Mark Comstock

Editor's note: This article is similar to one by the same author that begins on page 89. This version contains additional information about the defensive system that will be more appropriate for teams playing at higher levels of competition.

OUR DEFENSIVE philosophy is simple. We try to force our opponents to play out of their comfort zone or normal style with our man-to-man pressure defense.

We use these principles in teaching our defense:
1. Intelligent pressure on the ball.
2. Total or pressure denial one pass away.
3. Always have players from the help side cover up penetration.
4. Full-fronting of the post.
5. Dive and rotation on ball penetration.
6. Total commitment to conversion.

INTELLIGENT PRESSURE

Stress to your players the need to have pressure on the ball. If opposing players are allowed room to work, they'll pick the defense apart with high-percentage passing and shooting. Keep good pressure on the ball at all times to play effective man-to-man pressure defense.

The main points for putting pressure on the ball are:
- ✔ No fouls when pressuring.
- ✔ Discourage penetration.
- ✔ Use proper hand position to deflect passes.
- ✔ Force the offensive player to pick up the dribble, then "trace ball."
- ✔ Defenders must use three stances when defending the ball: stick (with dribble), point (dribbling) and trace ball (dribble picked up).
- ✔ "Jump" on all passes in the direction of the pass and "deny" or "help."
- ✔ Make people go over or under, never through you.

PRESSURE DENIAL

All five defensive players must be ready to deny the ball. The most important denial rule is to see both the ball and the assigned opponent at all times. Don't have your players open up to the ball. A player denies a pass to the offensive player by being "belly up."

When a player cuts behind the defender, "quick head" or turn the head over the shoulder to find the ball and deny the pass.

Also, deny guard-to-guard passes to put added pressure on the opposing guards. Many coaches might argue about using this tactic, but it has been an effective strategy for us.

Aggressive denial forces opponents into errors by disrupting their timing, forcing them farther out on the floor and making them play out of their comfort zone.

The main points for total or pressure denial defense when the pass is one player away are:

- ✔ Don't allow the quick reversal.
- ✔ Force the player to the back door or to vacate his or her position.
- ✔ Open up when the defender clears the lane.
- ✔ Deny high-post position on the ball side.
- ✔ Force the lob.
- ✔ Be ready for "X-ing" and rotation.
- ✔ Be ready to defend two-player plays.
- ✔ Communicate. Know what to say and when to say it.
- ✔ Understand "jump" to help or deny.
- ✔ You are not responsible for help-and-recover adjustments.

CONSISTENT HELP

To play pressure defense, you must have consistent help or your team will not be as aggressive as it could be. Players must feel that even if their assigned player gets behind them or penetrates, they still will not get scored upon.

The help-side player must be aware of his or her defensive assignment so that if the offensive player flashes to the basket, the help-side player doesn't give the offense an easy outlet or quick reversal.

The help-side player must be ready and in position to help and deny. The help-side player is the catalyst in a successful man-to-man defense.

Always have players in the help position if the opposing player is two passes removed from the ball and keep the player and ball in sight at all times.

- ✔ Be ready to deny the offensive player if he or she flashes. Keep hands up to avoid foul calls after the defender has checked the offensive player with the body to deny the pass. The defender must stick with the offensive player after the pass is denied.
- ✔ Be ready for crossing and rotation.
- ✔ "Leave and level" help 1 penetration at the foul line. "Leave and level" help 2 penetration is one or two steps outside the lane area.
- ✔ Take the charge. Have knees bent, hands up and grunt. Sell the charge to officials.
- ✔ Close-out short or long technique is critical.
- ✔ Make "help stops" from "help 1 or 2."
- ✔ Anytime the ball is dribbled, your entire defense should be thinking "help."

FRONT THE POST

To stay consistent with your pressure, make every attempt to keep the ball out of the low post by full-fronting the offensive post player. You want to force the lob pass and rely on ball pressure and help players create turnovers or discourage the attempt to complete a lob pass.

The post defender must be active to get in the full-fronting position and get over the top to help.

DIVE AND ROTATION

Whenever you get penetration with the pass or dribble, all players must dive and rotate using a technique called "X-ing."

X-ing describes the pattern players make on the floor. They should cross paths.

The main points for dive and rotation are:

✔ On a pass or dribble penetration, all players dive and force the ball back out.
✔ Rotate. It is the toughest play to make, but winners make it.
✔ "Scramble." The rule of the closest player to the ball applies.
✔ "Close-out" techniques should be short and long.

CONVERSION RULES

Play five-on-five situations as much as possible during a game. The main points for conversion are:

✔ 1 must stay back.
✔ 2 must remain level with the ball.
✔ 3, 4 and 5 sprint half the court; must "see ball."

Diagrams 1 through 7 illustrate player assignments in a pressure defense.

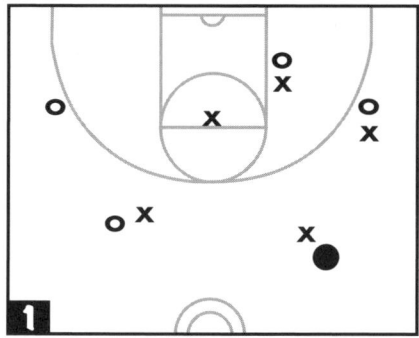

Diagram 1: Proper guard position. Notice the opposite defensive guard is in denial position.

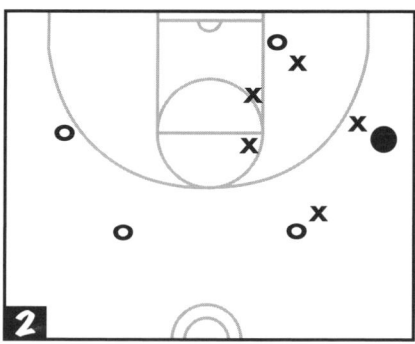

Diagram 2: Shows defensive assignments when the ball is pushed into the defensive forward position. Have the weak-side player in a help 1 or help 2 position to stop penetration by meeting the offensive player outside the lane area.

Deny the ball into a flashing post and full-front the post. Anytime the ball gets into the lane by a pass or dribble, the opponent has penetrated the defense. All five players dive into the lane area, force the ball back out and re-cover their original opposing players or defend an open player.

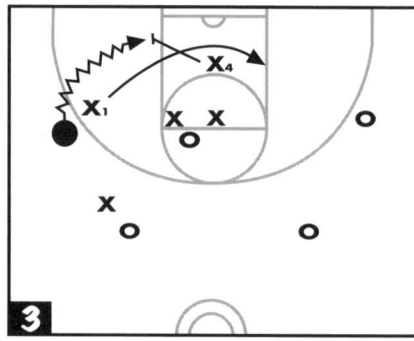

Diagram 3: Whenever the offense penetrates the defense, use X-ing and rotation.

This diagram shows baseline penetration and weak-side help from X4. X4 crosses (X-ing) with X1.

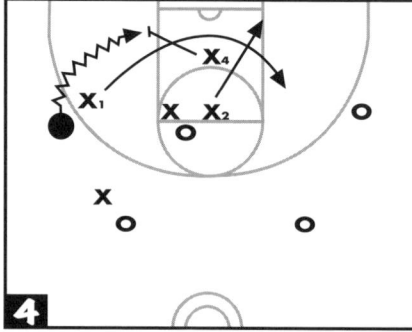

Diagram 4: Double X-ing occurs when X2 beats X1 to cover X4's original assignment. In that case, X1 continues up to find an opponent — probably X2's assigned player. This is double X-ing with rotation.

Diagram 5: Triple X-ing takes place if X3 picks up X2's assignment.

Diagram 6: Another technique that must be followed is having the strong forward (X1) resist coming off his or her player to defend the guard on dribble penetration.

The weak-side forward (X4)

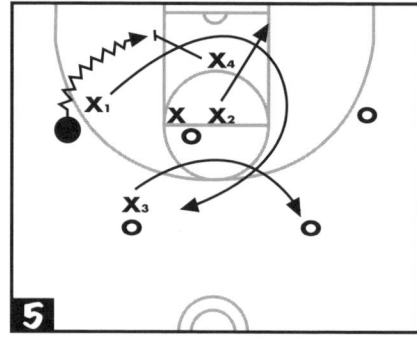

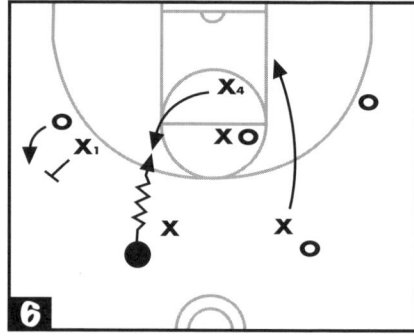

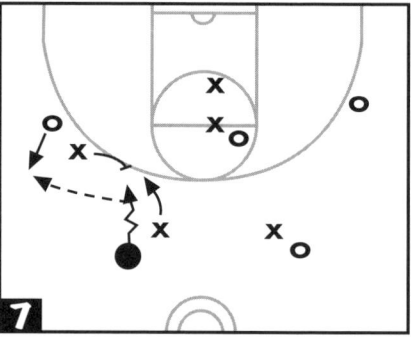

must help and cross with the player guarding the ball.

Diagram 7: The strong-side forward must stay with his or her defensive assignment and deny so the offense can't kick the ball back out for a jumper.

The weak-side help must come early or it will be wasted. Help on guard penetration must be outside the lane area with weak-side help coming in both situations.

Man-For-Man Multiple Defense
By Jim Baggot

TO HAVE A winning basketball team, you must defend against all offenses. The helping man-for-man defense is the one that comes closest to handling this assignment.

You can do anything with a helping man-for-man defense that you can do with a zone defense — sag against a tall or cutting and driving team, pressure good shooters outside, double or play in front of big post players, press a poor ball handling team, or pressure a control team and force a faster tempo.

Our basic defense is an assigned man-for-man with aggressiveness in switching on lateral movements by the guards. We stay with the assigned opponent unless picked off by a positive block. If we are picked off, we try to force over the top or slide through expecting help on a half or full switch.

Here are the basic positioning rules used to set up our defense, with tips on playing man-for-man defense against various offenses.

POSITIONING

Diagram 1: Overplay the opponent's strength. Position yourself so you can harass your opponent at all times. Try to keep the ball outside the defense. If it gets inside, jam and force it back outside.

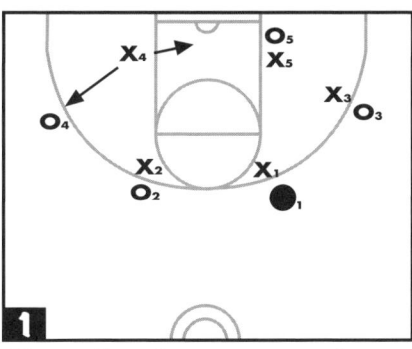

Never allow the opponent to handle the ball within the area around the free throw lane. Play the ball tough within 21 feet of the basket. Sag off any offensive player screening away from the ball and yell to your teammate to look out for "block" or "pick."

COVERING THE PIVOT

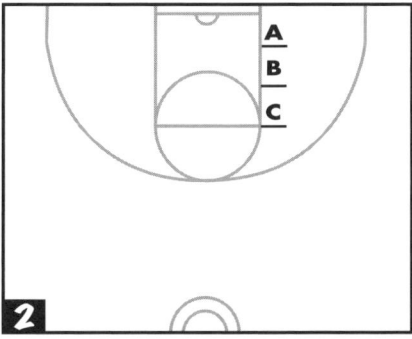

Diagram 2: The ball must not be allowed in the pivot area. If the offensive post player sets up low (area A), play in front to the ball side, behind on the weak side. If the offensive post player sets up half way (area B) play in front or 3/4 to ball side. If the

offensive player sets high (area C) play behind or 3/4 to ball side.

GUARD PLAY

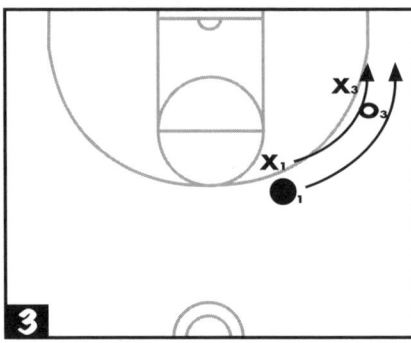

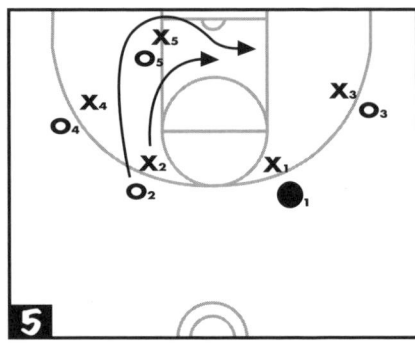

BOXING OUT FOR REBOUNDS

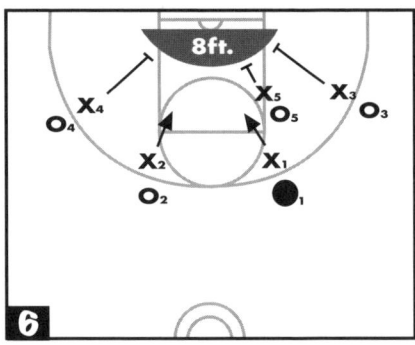

Diagram 3: Your guards must always stay between their opponent and the basket when the player they are guarding has the ball. They should stay between their opponent and the ball when they are cutting or moving without the ball. They must continually harass the opponent, never letting them do what they want to do.

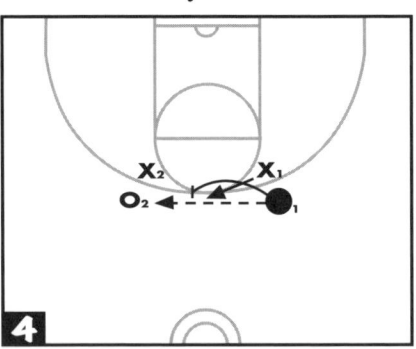

Diagram 6: After the shot is taken, the defensive forwards and center (X3, X4 and X5) initiate their box out about 8 feet in front of the backboard. The guards (X1, X2) recover long rebounds around the free throw area while boxing out the offensive guards.

DEFENDING VARIOUS OFFENSES

TANDEM POST

Diagram 4: This diagram illustrates how to make aggressive switches on positive blocks or when offensive guards weave or pick for each other.

Diagram 5: This is an example of the defensive guard staying between the ball and their opponent on diagonal or shuffle cuts off the ball.

Diagram 7: Defensive post players must stay in position or switch, which ever seems best (this can be determined by scouting reports). X1 must force 1 to one side, trying to keep them away from the strong side.

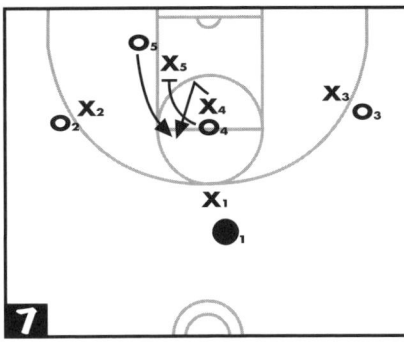

SHUFFLE

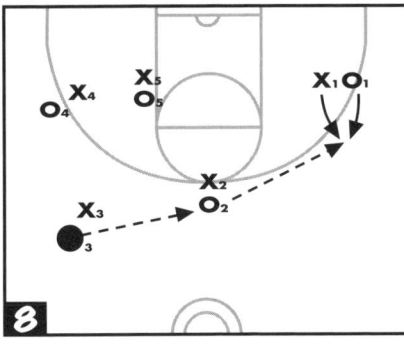

Diagram 8: Always press a team using the shuffle offense, since it's essentially a ball control offense. Force 1 very wide to receive the entry pass. Try and force the offense into a running game—normally they are not in proper physical condition for it.

SINGLE POST

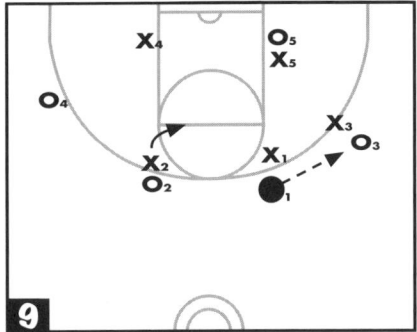

Diagram 9: X1 must harass 1 while X3 and X5 cover their men tight—they must stay glued. X2 can sag on a pass to 3. X4 sags to help where needed. In general, the team must follow the individual coach's standard rules of post defending.

DOUBLE-POST

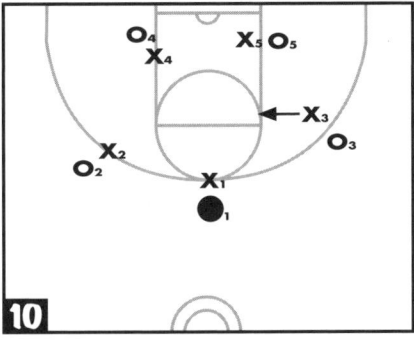

Diagram 10: The defense must continually try to force the ball to one side. Never allow a double-post team to operate from the center of the court. Overplay on one side (X1, X2 and X4) and sag off on the other (X5, X3) to accomplish getting the ball to one side. You can switch the overplay side each time down the floor or have a set pattern tailored to your defensive personnel or offensive teams strengths.

Set Defense

Man-To-Man Pressing Defense
By Pat Sullivan

JOHN WOODEN ONCE said "My philosophy of defense is to keep the pressure on an opponent until you get to his emotions."

The purpose of our man press is to tire our opponent's guards, both physically and emotionally, so they are not at their best at the end of the game.

On every possession, your players should make your opponent work just to get the ball up to half court to begin their offense.

✔ Play 10 players every game to maintain this constant full-court pressure.

✔ If your players can do this for an entire game, your opponent's tired legs and minds may create poor shots and poor passes in the game's final minutes.

KEY CONCEPTS

A key concept is that your players are not trying to steal the ball. Instead, they are trying to turn the ball carrier in the backcourt and make him change directions two or three times. If your defense does this on every possession, your opponent's players will be tired and unable to be at their best during the game's final minutes.

Vince Lombardi used to say: "Fatigue makes cowards of us all."

POINTS OF EMPHASIS

The following represent the points of emphasis you should stress to your players when they are guarding the ball in the back court. Teach both an ideal technique that you would like to see them use and a realistic technique.

✔ **How close should your defenders get to the ball handler?**
Ideal: Touch chest.
Real: Depends on the quickness of the ball handler and their proficiency with the ball in relationship to the defender's quickness.

✔ **Hands.**
Ideal: Inside hand on the ball; outside hand in the passing lane.
Real: Keep both hands outside and use the arms as pistons to drive the feet more quickly.

Time the rhythm of the dribbler with the defender's inside hand.

Teach your players to reach for the ball with their inside hand only in the last quarter.

✔ **Feet.**
Ideal: Don't cross your feet while defending.
Real: Do cross, especially when you get beat.

✔ **Eyes.**
Ideal: Watch the ball.
On change of direction dribbles, the ball gets there first, then the body.

✔ **Head.**
Teach your players that they must get their head to the ball to force the change of direction.
If the defender's eyes are on the ball, that will help get the head there.

✔ **Decisions.**
Get your defenders to turn the ball carrier in the back court.

Somewhere close to midcourt, the defenders must make the decision as to when to stop turning the ball carrier and force them to the side.

While one defender is guarding the ball carrier, have your remaining players in position to deny the pass on the ball side or give support to the defender guarding the ball on the help side.

Using "Junk" Defenses To Negate Talent Differential
By Kenny Edwards

A HIGH SCHOOL basketball coach is often faced with what people term a "rebuilding" year. In this situation, the team may be made up of younger, less-talented players than in the previous seasons. It can also mean the team is made up of a different type of player altogether (short and quick players as opposed to tall and slow).

Regardless of the change or difference, the coach is still faced with a huge dilemma: how to be competitive every night against a superior opponent.

Understanding that the basic foundation of any defensive system is a strong man-to-man, this article offers you a different perspective by detailing the primary functions of combination or "junk" defenses in overcoming talent differential.

A combination, or "junk," defense can be defined as having several players playing man-to-man defense while the remainder play a zone defense.

Examples of a combination defense are triangle and two, box and one, diamond and one and tandem and three defenses.

WHY A "JUNK" DEFENSE?
Take Away One Player

The primary function of a combination defense is to take the opposing team's "star" player out of the game.

By forcing the opponent's other players to score, the less-talented team is making opposing players do things they are not accustomed to doing or have not practiced. In addition, the "star" player often becomes frustrated and resorts to taking bad shots in order to score the usual amount of points.

As the coach of the less-talented team, consider rotating fresh defenders on the "star" player. This will wear the "star" player down, as they will use up a lot of energy just trying to get open. If the game remains close, especially late in the fourth quarter, you'll often see the other four offensive players sense their offense being off-balance, begin to panic and force bad shots because they realize scoring must come from different players.

Control Tempo

The second function of a combination or "junk" defense is to control the tempo of the game.

If the less-talented team gets back on defense quickly, the more-talented team is forced to abandon its up-tempo style of offense and slow down to work for a high percentage shot. This can be especially true if the "star" player is defended full court and denied the basketball.

By controlling the tempo, the opponent will get fewer shots. A premium is placed on the shots they take, their offensive motion may become broken, they become stagnant and resort to one-on-one moves.

Once the tempo is controlled by the less-talented team, the opponent begins to play the clock. Herein lies the old coaching adage: "Keep the game close until there are only 2 minutes remaining and find a way to win."

Make Them Think

The third function of the combination defense is to confuse the opposing players and coaching staff.

As a coach, you should realize that it may take the opposing players and coaches two or three possessions to identify the combination defense you're employing.

Sometimes the defense doesn't have to be very good, as just the appearance of a "junk" defense is enough to confuse the opponent and create fear and apprehension.

Most teams do not practice against a "junk" defense. Many coaches use the philosophy of "we'll just use our man-to-man offense." While this may work sometimes, it's not a sure-fire method, especially under the pressure situations of the fourth quarter.

Change Momentum

The fourth function of combination defenses is by using these defenses, you can change the momentum of the game very quickly.

As the defensive coach, you can pick and choose when and for how long to use a combination defense, allowing you to capitalize on momentum swings.

One of the best times to use a "junk" defense to change momentum is late in the game. Often it causes the opposing coach to call a time-out, or substitute unintelligently.

The coach may lose their composure briefly, causing doubt in the minds of the players. This may be enough to give the less-talented team the advantage it needs to win.

As the coach of a less-talented team, you owe it to the players, parents and the school to find a way to be competitive in every game. "Junk" defenses can often be the difference for two or three possessions, which may decide the outcome of the game.

Special Situation Defense: Tandem And Three
By Peter J. Grimes

AFTER LISTENING TO hundreds of coaches discuss defensive strategy, some common elements are constant.

✔ Even with the shot clock, a good defensive team keeps pressure on the ball and does not allow "free walks up the court."
✔ Zone defenses do not always shut down the opposition's highest scoring player.
✔ It is easier to limit the opponent to one shot by blocking out, but it is tougher to do so from a zone.
✔ Teach your team to be smart and play "ball" or "help" defense. It is imperative to stop the ball, not just your assigned opponent.

Trying to figure out what is the proper defense to employ is difficult. Should you change defenses during a game? Should a good team play a variety of traps, zones, etc.? If you have more talent than the opponent, should a pressure man-to-man defense be used throughout the game?

After playing, coaching and officiating on the high school and college levels for 27 years, it seems the best defense is the match up with man-to-man principles because it results in plenty of help, communication and is easier to run than most defenses.

High school teams change from year to year and players come and go more often, making it difficult to implement sophisticated defensive strategies.

We mostly employ a man-to-man pressure defense throughout the game and the Tandem and Three is a breath of fresh air. This defense confuses the opponent, which often can't tell if it's a man-to-man or a zone. Our best exhibition of this defense was when we went into a much stronger Division I team's gymnasium and held its high-powered offense to 35 points. This shocked many observers.

Because some high school teams tend to depend on one or two (maybe three) players to do the bulk of the scoring, a defense must stop those players. If a team has a

BALL/TANDEM LOCATION

Diagram 1: Tandem players "rotate" toward the ball playing any opponent in their area who is one pass/step or two passes/steps away.

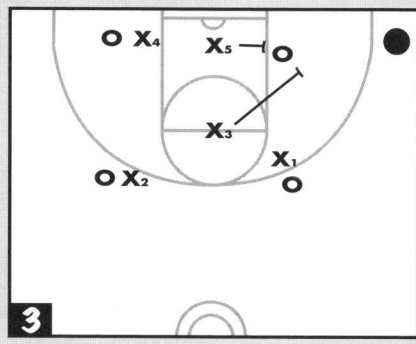

Diagram 3: Unless your tandem denies the post player, chances of cross-court passes to the corner shouldn't exist. But those are the types of passes you hope the offense will risk.

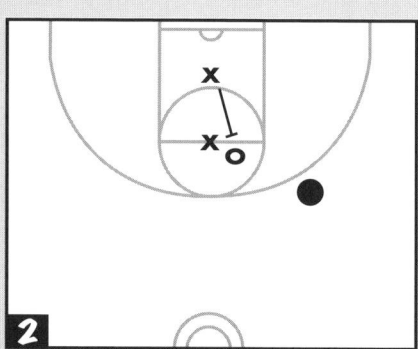

Diagram 2: Both tandem players shadow the post, with the top defender looking to prevent a pass to any cutter. Often, you challenge the offense to take the outside shot.

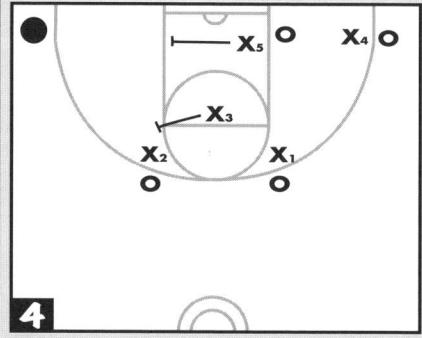

Diagram 4: Both tandem defenders must be active in boxing out duties to be successful.

dominant rebounder, you may assign a player to deny or box that rebounder. The basic idea of this defense is to make the opponent's fourth, fifth or sixth best player beat you.

But if you are playing a well-balanced team, this particular defense may not be the best choice.

TANDEM

The foul line player will be the best defensive "helper" guard or small forward. We call it the "help defender" or the "influencer." Just as in a fast-break, three-on-two situation, this player must stop the ball from penetrating the defense.

Points Of Caution: Teams that swing the ball cross-court, especially corner to corner, can give this defense fits. Teams that have a big player who requires frequent double-teaming can also be trouble.

Coaches may use this defense as a "situation defense" and save it for certain teams or game situations. Often, this defense will "give" perimeter jump shots to the players the defense selects.

The top tandem player must be quick and aggressive and play the angles. This defense will make a good man-to-man team better and serve to confuse most offenses.

TANDEM SET DIAGRAM

In this sequence, offensive players 1, 2 and 3 are being denied with man-to-man principles. The tandem rotates toward the ball with the foul line defender playing "the stopper." This forces 4 and 5 to handle the ball more than they expect.

> ### THE RULES OF THE DEFENSE ARE:
>
> **A.** Totally deny the offense's best scorer. Often quick, hard-nosed guards can cover taller opponents because help will come in the form of a tandem in the paint area.
>
> **B.** Keep constant pressure on the point guard and deny a pass back to that player once he or she gives up the ball.
>
> **C.** Take away the offense's second best player, scorer or rebounder and play tight man-to-man defense to deny this player.

Unique Features Make The 1-2-2 Zone Adaptable To Any Opponent
By Duane Estep

OUR GIRLS' VARSITY coaching staff worked hard on developing a unique series based on the 1-2-2 defense. The result of our efforts is what we call the 50 Lion defense.

We execute our 1-2-2 defense in several ways. First, we play a regular 1-2-2 set. Second, we move our big girls out front. Third, we "jump" in our 50 Jump and occasionally we trap out of all three sets.

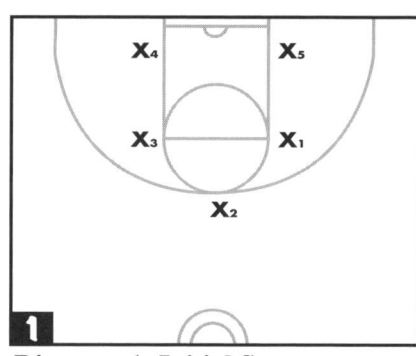

Diagram 1: Initial Set.

Set Defense

50 REGULAR

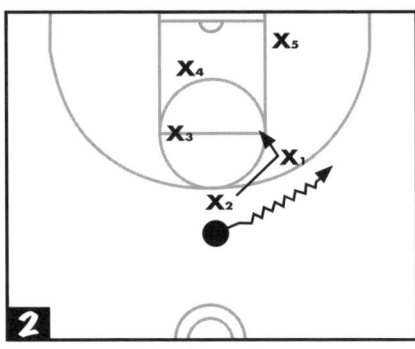

Diagram 2: 50 Regular.
We play our 2 guard up top to pressure the ball and drive it sideline. We place our 1 guard (usually our best defender) on the opponent's dominant side. 1 picks up the ball as 2 drops in to the elbow. 5 fronts and both 3 and 4 drop to the help side.

50 BIG

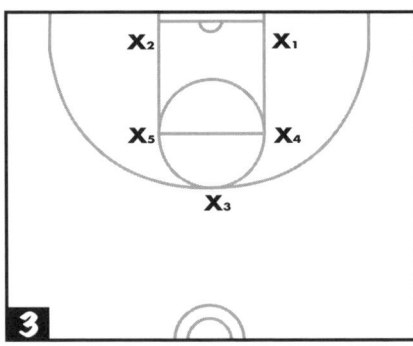

Diagram 3: "50 Big Initial Set".
Over the course of two seasons, we discovered a benefit in playing our post players out front in the 1-2-2 set. We found that we could disrupt the perimeter game of our opponents. It was difficult for our opponent's smaller guards to shoot and pass over our big girls.

We play our X3 up top to pressure the ball. X4 forward plays the opponent's strong side of the floor. We protect X5 by putting that player on the weak side. X1 (best rebounder) plays the strong block, while X2 plays the weak block.

KEYS TO 50 BIG

✔ Teach your post players to maintain a cushion on defense so the smaller guards can't penetrate easily.
✔ Teach your guards interior play.
✔ Have your post players get down, bend their knees and move their feet on defense to avoid fouls.
✔ Switch in and out of this defense to confuse opponents.

50 JUMP

Diagrams 4, 5: 50 Jump.
In our "Jump" version of the 1-2-2, we switch defensively in a zone.

X1 picks up the ball and forces baseline.

X5 jumps out on the ball and X1 crashes the block to cover the area that has been vacated by X5.

X4 must cheat over to cover for X1.

X3 must cover the weak side.

We have found that most guards will see X5 vacate the block and they will try a lob or bounce pass on the baseline side giving X1 a chance to steal as X1 crashes the block.

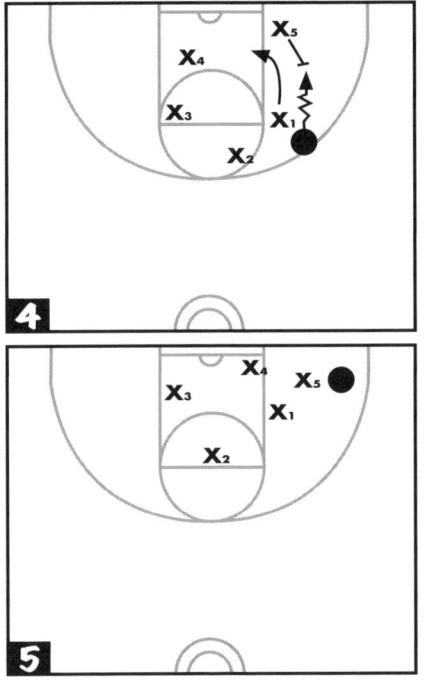

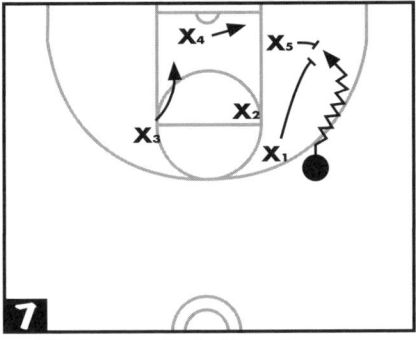

X1 forces the ball to the corner.
X5 jumps out to trap with X1.
X4 covers the low post.
X3 covers the weak side.
X2 covers the middle and the wing.

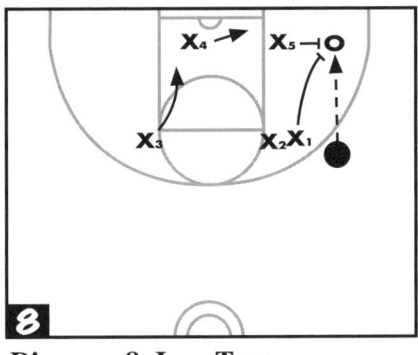

50 TRAP

We will occasionally trap out of our 50 series. We trap in several ways:

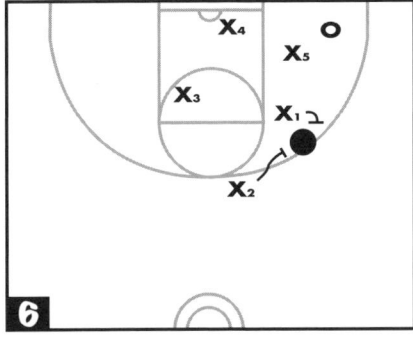

Diagram 6: High Trap.
X2 drives the ball, then traps with X1.
X5 cheats to cover the corner.
X4 cheats to the low post and X3 covers the middle.

diagram 7: Low Trap.
Dribble into corner.

Diagram 8: Low Trap.
Pass to corner.
X1 forces the pass to the corner, then moves to trap with X5.
X2 denies the pass to the wing area.
X4 covers the low post while covers the middle and weak side.

Diagram 9: Low Trap.
Pass to corner with cutter.
X1 forces pass to corner, then moves to trap with X5.
X2 covers the cutter until X4 picks up the move to the middle
X3 covers the weak side.

Set Defense

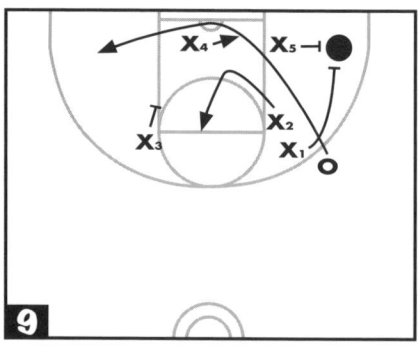

We realize we give up a little territory in our 50 Trap, but if we are trapping, we're gambling and trying to force the action.

FINAL THOUGHTS

We are an aggressive team defensively and we press often because we like to dictate the action. We will also mix up our 50 series throughout the game.

By mixing it up, you keep your opponents on their heels.

The biggest key to our 50 series is knowing your players' capabilities and adjusting the defense to them.

The "Gambler" 2-3 Trapping Defense
By Michael Smart

THE GAMBLER IS a 2-3 trapping quarter-court defense with some unique trappings. First, to employ it, it's imperative that a team have a big defensive presence inside. This defense actually allows the interior offensive players to receive the ball within the paint area.

To get most out of this defense, here are some necessities:
- ✔ Your team must have a big shot-blocking threat.
- ✔ Your four perimeter players must have quick hands and feet and exhibit excellent anticipation as they play the intercept position.
- ✔ The "Gambler" is ideal for a running, up-tempo game because of the turnover potential and the ability of this defense to produce a quick shot

by the opposition (we don't want to play defense very long).

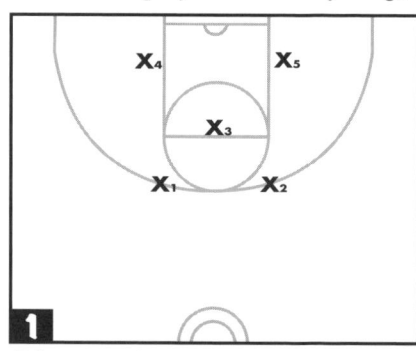

Diagram 1: The personnel and the location of your players in the 2-3 set may be determined by where you want your players in the offensive transition.

The following are the designations and assignments:

Defender X1: The release player or finisher; place your best one-on-one, open-court player in this position.

Defender X2: Should have quick hands and be a top defender, possibly a point guard.

Defender X3: The key to the defense! Plays behind the interior post player, and must be an intimidator and shot-blocker.

Defender X4: A top-notch rebounder.

Defender X5: A top defender, possibly a point guard.

Most teams attack right, so we prefer to have our best defenders at position X2 and X5. And since 55 percent to 60 percent of shots taken are rebounded inside the paint, we want our better rebounders in those spots.

If it's executed correctly, the "Gambler" offers four distinct advantages when used as a primary defense:

1. The opposition will not have attacked or faced a unique trapping defense such as this.
2. The opposition will typically attack this defense with three stationary perimeter players, making preparation easier.
3. This defense will shut down virtually all perimeter threats.
4. This defense will dominate a team with interior ball handling skills or weak interior play.

Diagram 2: The major adjustments of the "Gambler" are as follows: On the pass to the right wing, defenders X2 and X5 trap hard, with X3 playing a medium post position defensively-in line

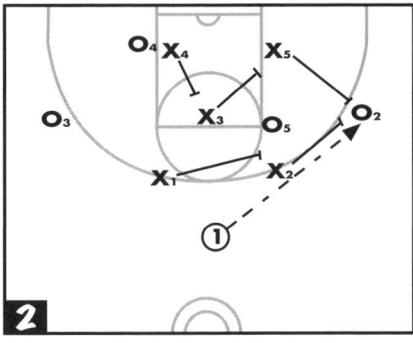

between the ball and the basket. The weak-side guard (X1) plays the intercept position between the high post (5) and maybe the low post (4), if 4 decides to cross over to the ball-side block.

Defender X5 also has an important responsibility. If the opposition, based on scouting information, has a tendency to send a player to the ball side corner, defender X5 must jump quickly from the wing trap to the baseline on the wing-to-corner pass. X5's job will be to defend the ball in the corner, and possibly trap the ball at the low block with X3, if the ball handler decides to penetrate.

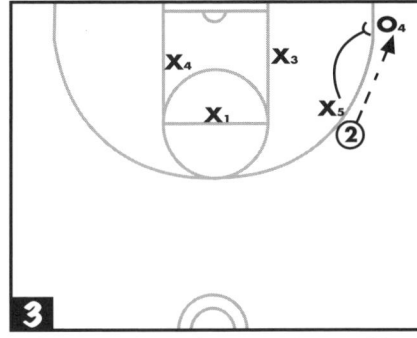

Diagram 3: Defender X3 should not wander toward the corner to trap with X5.

Set Defense

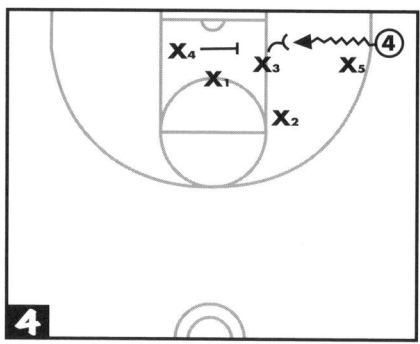
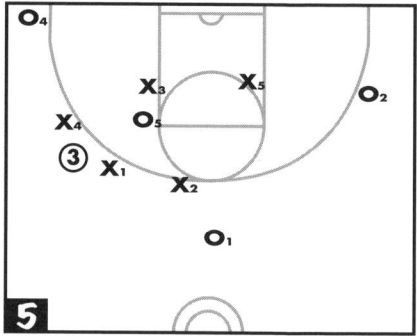

Diagram 4: X3 should wait until the ball is penetrated to the block area.

Once the ball enters the post, the perimeter defenders should double-down on the ball, hands digging. The perimeter defenders should never allow more than one post dribble without getting a steal or creating a loose-ball situation.

Diagram 5: If the ball is reversed to the opposite wing, defenders X1 and X4 become the trappers, and X4 becomes responsible for any pass to the ball side corner. Defender X2 becomes an interceptor then, splitting the high post and point guard, anticipating the pass by watching player 3's movements.

Anticipation, playing the passing lanes, inside intimidation, intercepting and aggressive trapping are all integral parts of the "Gambler" defense. Players also tend to respond more efficiently to something they enjoy doing, and kids love playing the "Gambler"!

Match-Up Defense Stymies Offenses
By Jason Wolfard

THE MATCH-UP DEFENSE is a defense based on simple man-to-man principles. The basic principle is that one player matches up hard on the basketball, and the others protect the lane while also matching up with other offensive players in their area.

Wherever the ball is on the key, the defense is usually matched up in a 1-3-1 set with a defender on the ball and a defender protecting the basket. Using this defense allows a team to use different strategies depending on the opponent.

BASIC RULES

In the match-up defense, basic goals or rules need to be set and understood. With these guidelines, a coach can tweak certain points in the defense for different strategies.

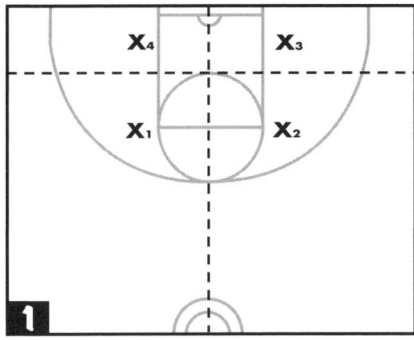

Diagram 1: Defensive Areas. Establish general areas that certain players are initially responsible for. As an offense moves, or as a coach sees fit, these areas can be adjusted.

RULE 1: The match-up defense is predicated on a partner system with the X1, X2, X3 and X4 players.

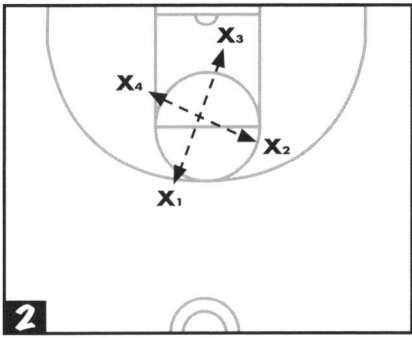

Diagram 2: In this defense, X1 and X3 are partners and X2 and X4 are partners. (X5's role will be discussed in a later rule.) In this partner system, when one player has the ball, that player's partner covers the basket. The player covering the basket should be low enough to see all the other players on the floor. The other two players line up on each side to take the next pass either way.

Although this partner system is the main one, another underlying partner system must be understood for lateral movement of the defense. This system involves X1 and X2 as partners and the X3 and X4 as partners. It usually applies when the ball has been passed to a wing position on the floor.

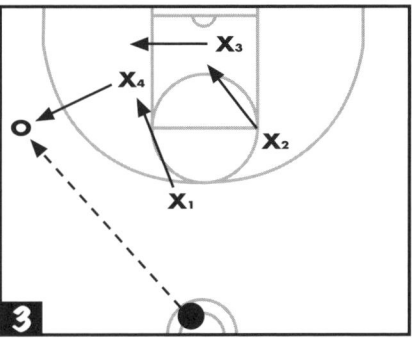

Diagram 3: When one player moves to take the pass, that player's partner must also move in order to cover that player's area. When both partner systems are applied simultaneously, the match-up defense has continuous movement, which is critical as the ball is moved.

When X4 guards the ball, X2 must cover the basket and X3 must move to where X4 previously was (low post). X1 drops to the high post.

RULE 2: *X5's Role.* X5 has a simple rule to follow, however, that player must move on every pass. X5 must point the ball to the basket while staying in the lane, but must play opponents differently depending on ball position.

Diagram 4: X5 is responsible for the area around the lane. When the ball is in the middle of the floor at the top of the key, X5 can play two

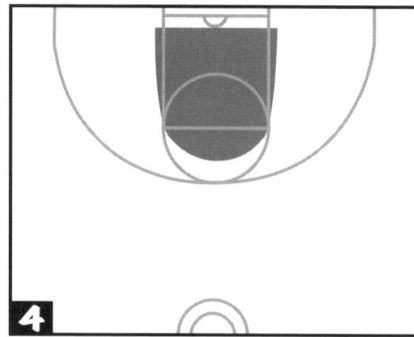

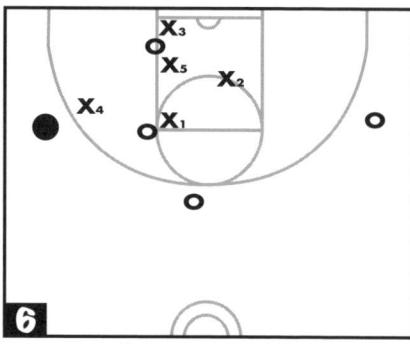

different positions. If there is not an offensive player in the high post area, X5 can play in the middle of the lane and cheat toward the low post. If an opposing player is in the high post, X5 must step up and play directly behind, to a side or try to dead front.

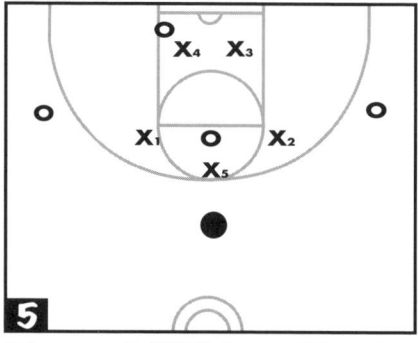

Diagram 5: If X5 fronts, X1 and X2 can play more toward the wing players.

Diagram 6: When the ball is at a wing position, X5 must play the topside of the low post denying an entry pass. X5 will have help on the low side from X3 or X4.

RULE 3: *Passing And Penetration.* This defense allows teams to fairly easily move the ball around the outside of the key. At times, your players can deny the next pass if necessary.

As the ball is moved around the key, the defenders protecting the lane must close out hard and quick on the ball while the others protect the lane. Penetration by an opposing player with the ball or via a pass can't be allowed.

When an opponent penetrates with the ball, the defenders must double-team and force the ball to be kicked back outside. On a penetrating pass, all five players must retreat to the lane with two or three players surrounding the opponent with the ball and forcing them to kick it back outside.

RULE 4: The ultimate goal in this defense is to allow an opponent one contested shot, and then the defense gets the rebound. All shots must be contested with a hand in the shooter's face.

The other four players must block off the lane area forming an umbrella around the basket. The player covering the basket must block out on the weak side. The player covering the high post must first block off the high post and then protect the top of the lane.

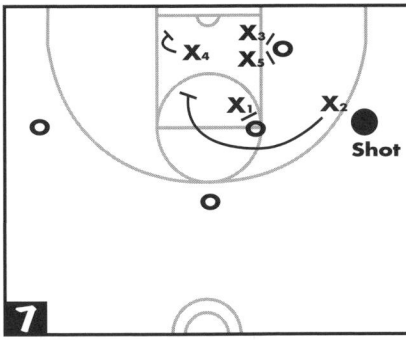

Diagram 7: Players covering the low post must block out the opponent they're covering (X5 blocking out the topside and the other player blocking out the low side). The player who contested the shot must retreat to the lane and block out in any open area.

SPECIAL SITUATIONS

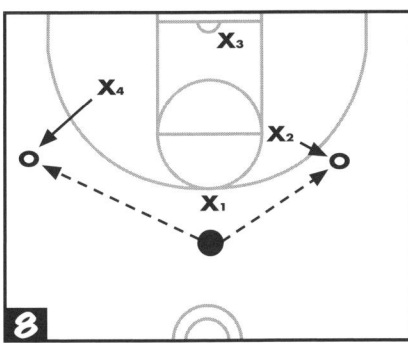

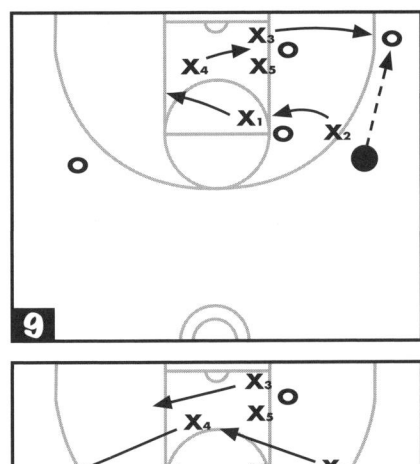

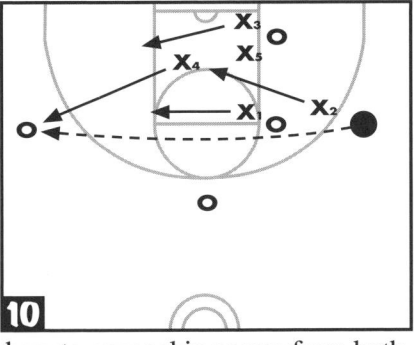

Diagram 8: Covering The Next Pass. When one player has the ball, the players to the right and left look to cover the next pass in either direction.

Diagram 9: Covering The Short Pass. When a pass is made from the wing to the corner, the low-side low-post defender must take the pass with the other defenders rotating respectively.

Diagram 10: Covering The Skip Pass. Your defense needs to know how to cover skip passes from both wing and the corner.

On a skip pass from the wing, X4 must take the ball with X3 retreating to the low post and X1 retreating to the high post on the ball side. X5 will cover the low post on the topside all the way across the lane. X2 will move to protect the basket.

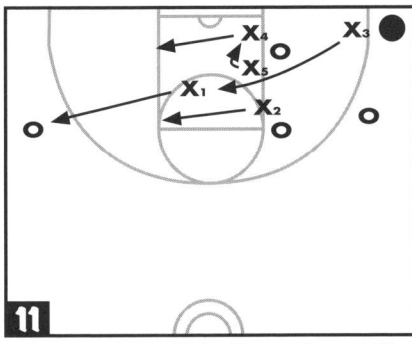

Diagram 11: Skip Pass From The

Set Defense   **119**

Corner. How this pass has to be covered depends on where it is going. This is probably the toughest pass to cover. When the pass is thrown between the high post and basket, the defender covering the basket must take the pass. This may force players to cover different areas as the defense rotates, but they will still find themselves diagonal from their partner.

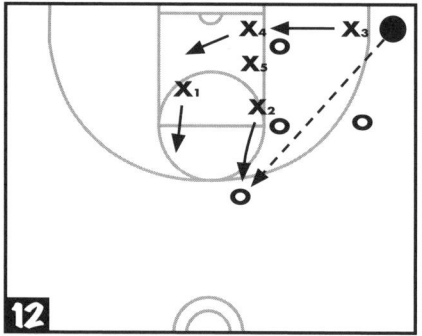

Diagram 12: When the pass is thrown in front of the high post defender, the high post must take the pass with all other defenders rotating respectively.

OTHER COVERAGES

Covering Cutters: If a cutter comes from the weak side and empties the weak side, the defender covering the basket must pick up the cutter and communicate with the other defenders until another defender can pick up the cutter.

If the weak side is empty, the defender covering the basket can cheat into another area and allow a teammate to move further out on another opponent.

The high post defender must deny high post flashes. The defender should face away from the baseline to see the flash occurring.

Covering Screens: On any screen, the defender getting screened must try to avoid the screen and move over the top of it. Other defenders must react accordingly.

When covering an opponent moving from the weak side to the strong side off a screen, the defender covering the basket must pick up the cutter all the way to the screen.

At that time, a jump switch must occur with the player getting screened going over the top (matching up with the cutter) and the player defending the basket who followed the cutter picking up the screener.

Covering A Low-Post Player. When the low post receives the ball, that player must be covered by the low post defender on the low side and X5 on the topside.

The defenders should form a V, staying between the basket and the player with the ball. Both defenders should put their hands up, forcing the low post to kick the ball back outside.

If that player puts the ball on the floor, the defender covering the player who made the entry pass must cover down hard.

PRACTICE DRILLS

These practice drills allow the perimeter defenders to see the different situations they might encounter.

Diagram 13: Shell Drill 1: This helps the four defenders understand

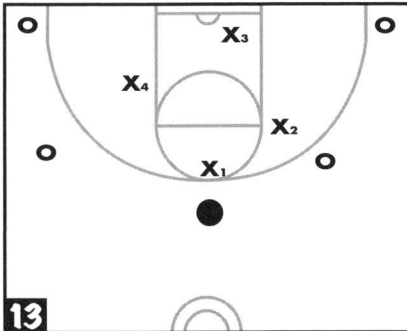

the correct rotation. Almost all possible situations are created during this drill.

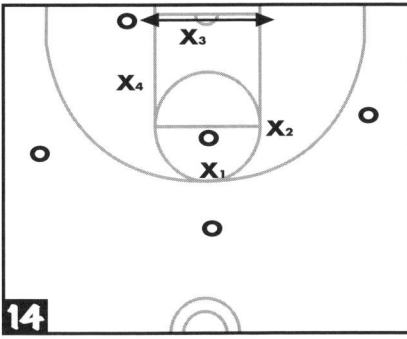

Diagram 14: Shell Drill 2: This drill teaches X1 and X2 how to retreat to the lane on a high post pass. X3 and X4 learn to cover an opponent in the short corner. You can also have the short corner defender flash to the high post so that your players learn how to communicate and deny the high-post flash.

5 Vs. 5 Live Drill: In this drill, have your offense go through screens, cutters and penetration so all five defenders learn how to cover each situation.

ADD EXTENSIONS

The match-up defense can be tweaked in many ways. Here are just some examples:

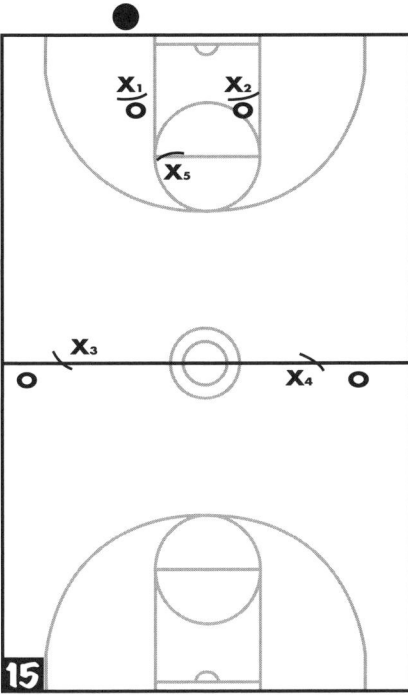

Diagram 15: Various Coverages. This defense can be extended all the way to a full-court, denial match-up. In the full court, X1 and X2 can front the two offensive players, X5 will play a center field position covering the inbound pass and X3 and X4 match-up man-to-man in the back court.

Denying The Pass: At any time, a defender can deny the next pass and force the offense to pass to another person.

Diagram 16: Trapping In The Half Court. Traps that can be used include trapping the dribbler crossing the half-court line.

Diagram 17: Trapping The First Pass Below The Free-Throw Line Extended. These are usually predetermined traps and throw an element of surprise at the offense.

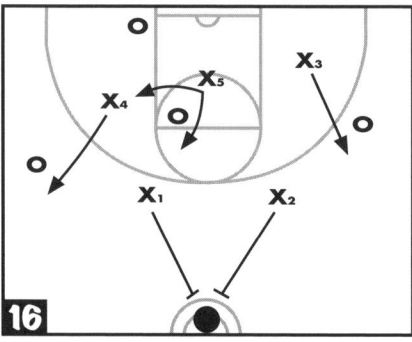
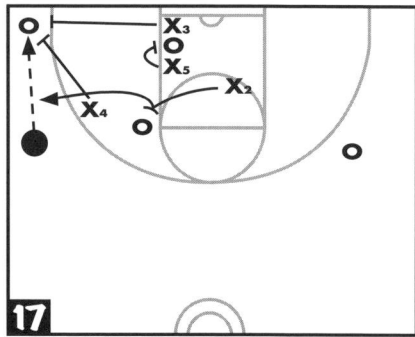

Note that defenders have taken about two steps up the floor.

EFFECTIVE, VERSATILE

The match-up defense can be adjusted to specific teams, styles and situations. If you can establish the basic rules and tweak your defense in certain spots, you'll find many teams will not be able to figure out the type of defense they are going against.

This defense allows a coach to manipulate it in different ways. Breaking down the defense in practice and bringing it back to the big picture will allow your players to apply this defense in any game situation.

Triangle And Two Defense
By Paul Basey

WE USE THIS defense anytime the opponent has a poor shooter in the game at the guard or small forward positions. We double-team one of the opponent's other players with the purpose of leaving their poorest shooter open.

This defense also works against teams with one or two outstanding offensive players that score the majority of their team's points, with the rest of the team filling in as role players. The triangle and two defense allows us to shut their "star" players down, requiring role players to step up and play beyond their capabilities.

ADVANTAGES

There are many advantages to running the triangle and two defense.

1. It's easy to understand. You can explain this defense in 20 minutes of practice and use it effectively the next day. Players will remember how to play it the whole season.

2. It will temporarily stop the other team's best players, whether

they're post players or guards. Only the opponent's weakest shooter is left open to shoot a short jump shot. As the coach, you dictate with defensive pressure who will shoot for the other team and who you will not allow to shoot.

3. It tests the opponent's coaching staff. Can they recognize the defense? Do they have the ability to quickly and properly adjust and attack this defense?
4. It can confuse an opponent, leading to frustration and a disruption in team chemistry. This often changes the momentum in your favor.
5. Most teams do not practice playing against the triangle and two defense. They rarely, if ever, face it during a game.
6. You are always in great rebounding position because of the triangle.

WEAKNESSES

There is one major weakness to the triangle and two defense. The scheme of the defense allows one offensive player to be open in the 15-foot range. If the player left open can knock down the short jumper consistently, your defense will break down.

But because you can alter the defense and choose which offensive player you are leaving open, this weakness is also an advantage on occasions.

POSITIONS, RESPONSIBILITIES

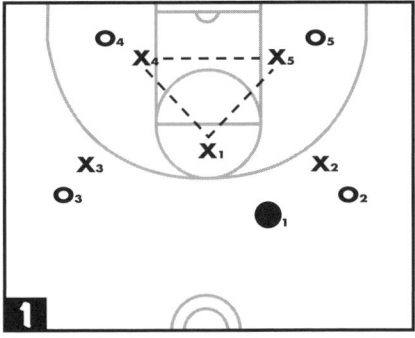

Diagram 1: Start with your post defenders, X4 and X5, guarding the low posts and your point guard X1 on the free-throw line. This is the triangle.

X2 and X3 will be playing man-on-man defense on the opponent's best two guards. X2 and X3 should always be in total denial position — never playing help side, never switching — following their player everywhere. If their player gets the ball, X2 and X3 should take away the baseline.

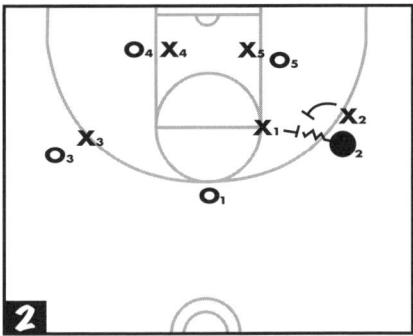

Diagram 2: X1 is the designated double-teamer. When the ball is on either wing, regardless of who has the ball, X1 should move to the high post with one foot on the cor-

ner and one foot below the free-throw line.

X1 will double-team the ball handler if 2 tries to penetrate on the dribble, but only if 2 tries to dribble penetrate.

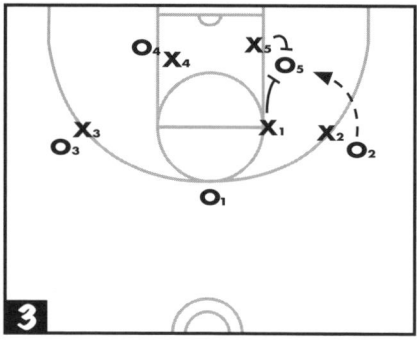

Diagram 3: If the ball is passed into the post, X1 will immediately slide down the lane and double-team. X5 should establish a half-front position below 5, with X1 moving to a half-front position from above.

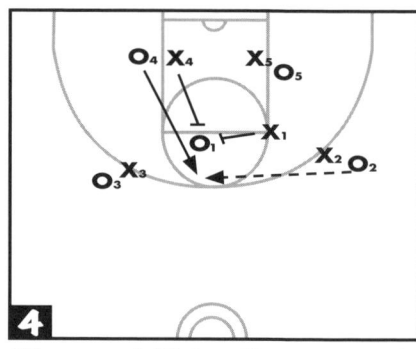

Diagram 4: If the offense moves 4 to the high post, X4 can come up to offer help. If the ball is passed to 4, X4 and X1 can double-team 4, but only do it in extreme situations. It's better to keep X4 in the post as much as possible.

23 Jump Defense
By Dick Luther

THE 23 JUMP defense can give a different look to your 2-3 zone defense and be very effective. In any zone, coverage is essential. Players will play with added confidence if the zone coverage is totally understood.

Diagram 1: 2-3 Zone Coverage.

Your defense must cover the low and high post, and the weak side of the zone.

Spring the jump at anytime — a set call, after a time-out, start of the second half or for that matter, the start of the game.

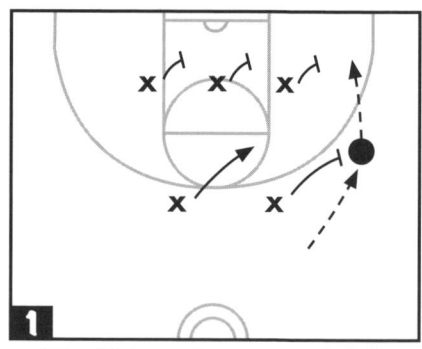

The 23 jump becomes a 1-1-3 set (extended half court).

Diagram 2: 1-1-3 Half-Court Set

The point guard (X1) attacks with man-to-man pressure on the

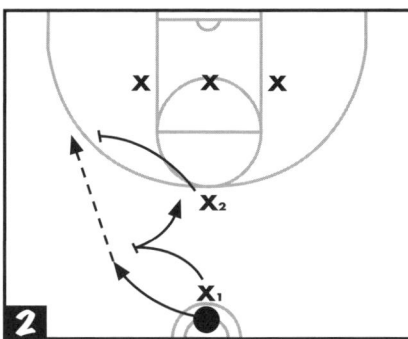 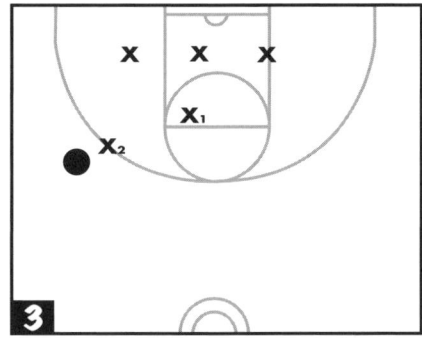

dribbler at half court. X1 works on stopping the ball or forcing the ball to the sidelines. On the first pass, X2 covers the pass and X1 sinks back into zone coverage.

Diagram 3: Aggressive 2-3 Set
Your defense is now back into a 2-3 set. Be very active and aggressive with your zone defenses.

1-3-1 Trapping Zone
By Wim Cluytens

MANY OF THE best European teams play some form of zone defense and certain teams are famous for their ferocious 1-3-1 zones.

In fact, in Belgium a team has won several national titles by utilizing this particular zone defense.

Players should learn to play man-to-man defense first before they learn to play zone.

ADVANTAGES OF 1-3-1 TRAP

1. Not many teams play this zone, so teams are not used to attacking this defense.
2. It's a very aggressive zone. Your players will always attack the ball and close passing lanes.
3. It can be played with any personnel. But the taller and quicker your players are, or the better they can execute the man-to-man defensive principles, the better this zone will function.
4. Although every spot of the zone needs specific characteristics, players can be interchanged. Every coach will have their own ideas on how to position their personnel.
5. We've seldom used this zone for an entire game. It's mostly used as a surprise element at the beginning or end of each half, after a time out or when we're behind. Your team can create confusion by mixing up the traps.
6. As with other zone defenses, your team can easily fast break out of the 1-3-1 zone.

7. By slightly changing the positioning of some players, you can defend nearly every offensive situation.
8. This zone works well against teams with very good guards or strong post players.
9. The trapping zone is easy for your players to understand. There are few rules and your players can quickly grasp the basics in a short period of time.

Stunting from this zone and refining the techniques comes quickly. Several breakdown drills will help your players learn these concepts.

PLAYING THE 1-3-1 ZONE

Diagram 1: Initial Set.

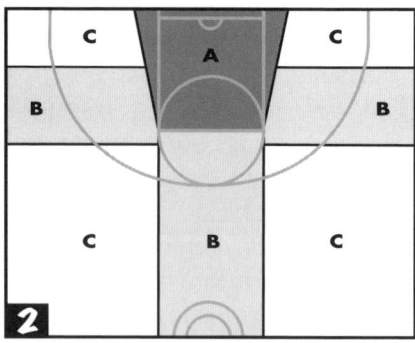

Diagram 2: Zones A, B And C.
Keep the ball out of zone B as much as possible. When the ball is in area B, have your team:
✔ Use man-to-man principles.
✔ Double-team from the free-throw line extended.
✔ Don't permit the ball to come into zone A. When this happens, force them out of that area as quickly as possible by double- and triple-teaming.
✔ In zone C, always put pressure on the ball. Your players can decide whether or not to double-team.

PLAYER CHARACTERISTICS

Because player positions are interchangeable, the numbers on the diagrams are not always the same as "normal" (offensive) numbers. Look at the characteristics of your players for this defense:

X1: Top Defender (Front Player).
✔ Normally this should be your point guard.
✔ Needs to be fast, aggressive and mobile.
✔ Should be a good defender against the dribble.
✔ If this player has size and long arms — that's ok. (I sometimes use my 2 at this spot.)

X3 And X4: Wing/Side Defenders.
✔ Should be good defenders with some size.
✔ X4 (the right wing) should be the best rebounder of the two (normally our 4, but sometimes 3 and even 5 can play here if they are faster or better rebounders).

X5: Middle Defender.
✔ Normally our 5 player. Should be a big, strong, very active rebounder.
✔ Sometimes we are forced to put our slowest and worst big defender here. This positioning has worked out well.

X2: Back Defender.
✔ Usually the 2 guard or smallest forward.
✔ Although it always helps to be a little taller, this defender must be quick, intelligent and possess good anticipation skills.

RULES FOR PLAYERS

Note: The positioning rules are only given as help for the players. They must be adapted to the way this zone is played at that moment or to the position of the opponents.

Playing between two spots can mean the body of the defender is in the possible passing line or that the player's hand can reach into the passing line. (This makes it seem like you are inviting the opposition to come into this area, which seems to be open but really isn't.)

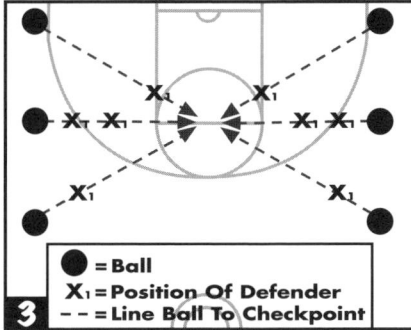

Diagram 3: Top Defender (X1)

✔ The top defender always plays between the ball and the center of the free-throw line.
✔ X1 picks up their assigned player at the midcourt circle and tries to keep that player from getting into zone B.
✔ X1 is free to double-team with X3 or X4 (at the free-throw line extended or even as a "stunt" in zone C).
✔ Has to box out high-post players on any shot from within the free-throw line.

Note: When double-teaming (X3 and X2) in the baseline corner or when the offense is playing with two high posts, X1 covers the strong-side elbow. When there is no double-teaming, cover the weak-side elbow.

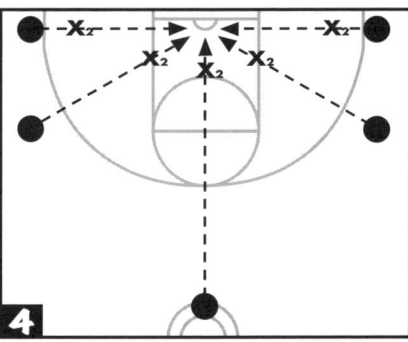

Diagram 4: Back Defender (X2)

✔ X2 always moves toward the ball side.
✔ Fronts everybody in the low-post area.
✔ Covers the player with the ball in the baseline corners.
✔ Stops all baseline drives without allowing a shot from the corner.
✔ Always boxes out assigned player.

Set Defense

- ✔ Double-teams the low post with X5.
- ✔ Plays help and recover defense on drives by the wing player.
- ✔ Helps guard against lob passes into the high post (when 5 should play in front of the post).

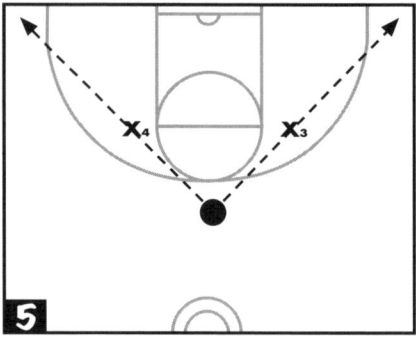

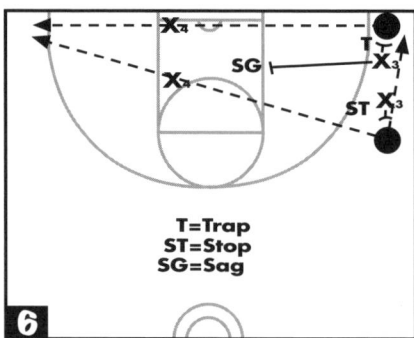

T=Trap
ST=Stop
SG=Sag

Diagrams 5 and 6: Wing Defenders (X3 and X4)
- ✔ The strong side wing player has the choice to trap or not with X1 at the free-throw line extended (or even higher in zone C when chasing the ball).
- ✔ When the ball is in the corner, the defender can trap with X2, deny the pass back to the strong-side wing offensive player or defend the paint. They must decide whether they will trap, stop or sag. (T = Trap, ST = Stop, SG = Sag)

- ✔ They can triple-team on very strong low-post players with X2 and X5.
- ✔ The weak-side defender plays on a line with the ball toward the weak-side corner with one foot in the lane. Do not allow skip passes into the corner.
- ✔ Because X5 plays in front of the low post, the weak-side defender helps on lob passes into the post.
- ✔ If there is a cross-court pass from the corner to the weak-side wing, wings should try to intercept it.

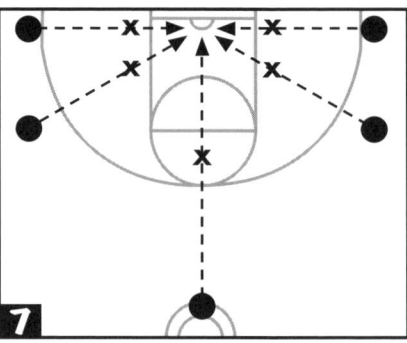

Diagram 7: Middle Defender (X5)
- ✔ X5 is "king of the bucket" — allowing no ball penetration (pass or drive).
- ✔ Fronts everybody in X5's zone, especially the low post and sometimes the high post.
- ✔ Double-teams at the baseline with X2 or X3, or triple-teams with them.
- ✔ Double-teams at the free-throw line with X2.
- ✔ Leaves the high-post area for the low-post area when a pass goes from the wing to the corner.

Using The "13" Zone Defense And Its Variations
By Mike Madagan

BECAUSE IT IS different, this "13" zone defense and its variations have worked very well for us. Here's why:

1. WHY SHOULD YOU CONSIDER USING AN EXTENDED ZONE?

A. Opposing teams must spend valuable practice time preparing for a defense they don't often see.

B. Most teams have a standard zone or man-to-man offense, but don't have a standard offense to use against an extended zone. Most end up in some type of standstill — which is usually a 2-1-2 set.

C. It gives you a change-of-pace defense that can give you a lift.

D. In our case, it gives us an identity. We have great pride in our extended zone defense and our players are sold on it.

E. Your team can fast break out of it very well.

2. WHEN TO USE AN EXTENDED ZONE

A. After made baskets or dead ball situations.

B. Against setup teams after missed or made shots — against some teams which press and still play an extended zone.

C. If it's not effective early in the game, come back to it later. Always use it at the start of the game to see what your opposition will do.

D. This zone is particularly effective if you get ahead, as the other team will have a tendency to be impatient.

E. Do not use it against all teams. Use it only against teams that feel you can beat without using a "special" defense. Avoid using this defense continually as you must vary your defenses.

3. DRILLS FOR TEACHING THE EXTENDED ZONE

A. We use very few drills in teaching this particular defense. Instead, we spend a great deal of time explaining positioning, responsibilities and working five players as a unit. Always talk responsibly and give your players more freedom.

B. Change around your drills, especially those that are used to show a player what to do after they have left their feet. A good example is a baseline drive.

C. Ball reaction drill for centers.

D. Shuffle drill with hands extended high over the head.

E. Constantly go back to the basics.

4. INITIAL POSITION OF THE PLAYERS

X1 Should be the biggest guard, and should be a good rebounder who is smart and can be given freedom. The player should pick up the ball at three-quarter court and force the ball to one side or the other. The ball should not be brought up the middle of the court.

X2 Quickest forward.

X3 Best rebounding forward.

X4 Smallest guard. He or she should be a quick, take-charge, hardnosed, out-front person who pressures the ball.

X5 Center.

5. DEFENDING THE BALL ON THE SIDE OF THE FRONT COURT AREA

X1 and **X2** form a passive trap on the ball, hoping to get a hand on an errant pass or force the ball to be thrown away or at least thrown high.

X3 is responsible for the entire area to the basket line.

X4 remains on baseline to the ball side of the foul line, must not cheat and only moves out when the ball is thrown.

X5 plays the high post man-to-man. If the post player remains low, they adjust accordingly. If there's no post player, play the post area being alert for a flashing post.

6. WHAT SHOULD BE DONE WHEN THE BALL IS SWUNG FROM GUARD TO GUARD?

The responsibilities are the same as listed previously, only mirrored.

7. WHAT SHOULD BE DONE WHEN THE BALL IS SWUNG INTO THE CORNER?

As the ball is swung into the corner, **X4** and **X2** should form a passive trap.

X5 moves to the low post area and **X1** drops to the foul lane.

X1 will be responsible for any player in the high post area.

X3 moves low away from the ball. It's extremely important that all players are aware of the passing lanes and force the ball to be thrown over the top of the defense. It's also very important to have constant communication by all players, especially as offensive players move in and out of the post area.

The weak side forward should become a quarterback for defense and can see everything when the ball is in the corner.

8. KEYS TO USING THE EXTENDED ZONE

A. The ball must not be allowed to go to "post" area.

B. Don't put too much pressure on the ball, but make it look like pressure.

C. Be aware of passing lanes and continually force the ball away from the basket.

D. Players must rebound. Since this is the biggest weakness with this defense, constantly go over rebound assignments. The front man is very important.

E. Force changes in the passing lanes. Force the ball over the top.

F. Preach to your players that they must move when the ball is thrown and not wait until it reaches the target.

9. EXTENDED ZONE VARIATIONS

A. With the 32 X defense, pick up players at three-quarter court.
   1. Nurse the ball up the court without really hard traps and simply extend the defense.

B. Scramble out of a "31" trap anywhere, which is usually around the mid-court area.
   1. This serves as an excellent change of pace.
   2. It can be called six or eight times per game.
   3. Use to pick up the pace of a regular defense if your players start standing around or get lazy.

C. 34-31 hard traps.
   1. The 34 defense is a 1-2-1-1 full-court zone press.

The Rotating 1-3 And Chaser Defense
By Kenny Edwards

SO CALLED "JUNK DEFENSES" have gotten a bad rap over the years. Still, the majority of coaches in the game today have some sort of combination defense to combat any opponent on any given night. In looking for a defense that would offer good rebounding coverage and still extend to the perimeter to cover an opponent's best shooter, I began experimenting with a 1-3 zone, and that's how the Rotating 1-3 and Chaser came about in our system. This defense is not for every team, but it works very well with the talent we have. One of the keys for us has been putting players in the right places.

Player positioning in this defense is very important. You must first identify your opponent's best perimeter player (usually their best shooter) and assign your best defender to guard that threat man-to-man. This defender must not be allowed to give help, except in extreme emergency situations. For the purposes of this article, X2 is assigned man-to-man responsibilities. Positioning of the other players is shown in diagram 1.

Player X1 is the point guard, who must be smart, quick and able to anticipate your opponent's passes. X1 starts out in the area between the free-throw line and the top of the key. Player X3 is the small forward, and starts out at the low block to the right of X1. This player must be fairly quick and a good rebounder. Player X4 is the big forward, who also must be a good rebounder. This player starts out at the low block to the left of X1. Player X5 is the center (usually your best rebounder), and starts in the middle of the lane and may extend up to the free-throw line.

As with every defense, there are certain situations when the Rotating 1-3 and Chaser is best utilized. These include:

1. When key members of your team are in foul trouble. Most of the time these are inside players, who can be "protected" in the 1-3 zone portion of this defense. If X2 is in foul trouble, then you may want to have that player switch positions with X1.
2. When you want to confuse your opponent. This may be a crucial spot, when any little momentum swing can decide the outcome of the game.
3. When you want to slow the tempo of the game. Should you decide not to switch to an all out zone, and you want constant pressure on one of your opponent's best players, this may be a viable option.
4. When your opponent can hurt you with only one perimeter player. In this case, the Rotating 1-3 and Chaser can help you determine who shoots the outside shot for the other team.

Diagram 1: The Rotating 1-3 and Chaser set is the same as that for a regular 1-3 and chaser. However,

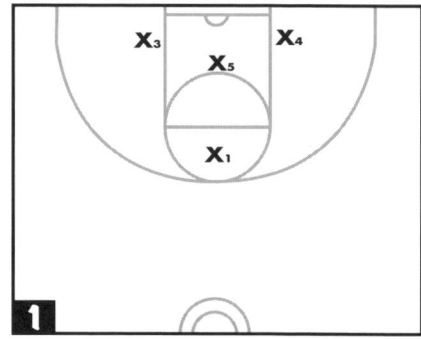

that's where the similarities end. As the ball moves, each player must be alert to the options of the other team and position accordingly.

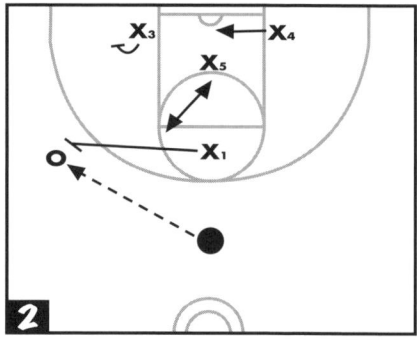

Diagram 2: If the ball is passed from the top of the wing, X1, who matched up on the ball at the top, follows the pass to the wing. If the wing chooses to penetrate before X1 arrives, then X5 should step up and stop penetration. X3 rotates on top of any low post player to prevent the entry pass into the ball side low post. X4 is in help-side position on any lob into the low post and still is in position to rebound the off side. X5 covers any flashes through the middle and the high post. This player has rebounding responsibility in the middle of the court.

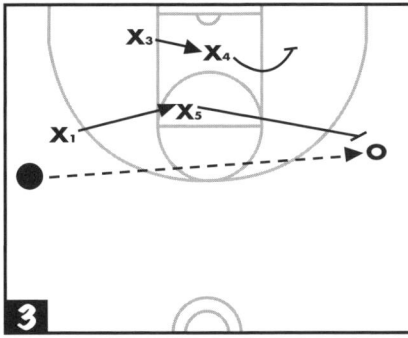

Diagram 3: The pass from the wing across to the off-side wing. This could also be the elbow-to-elbow pass of the Flex offense. On the pass, X1 sprints to the middle of the lane to cut off any quick flashers, and to "bump" X5 over to the ball. If X5 leaves too early, then the middle of the lane is open. X4 rotates around any low post sealing and gets in good denial defense on the ball-side low post. X3 rotates into help-side position in the lane. The rebounding responsibilities are now reversed, with X1 now assuming X5's role.

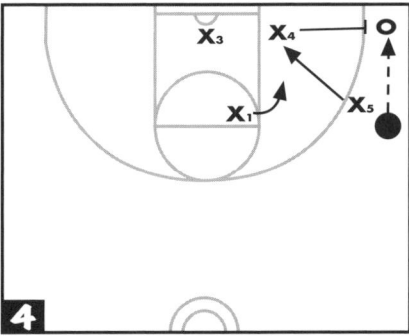

Diagram 4: The rotation for the wing-to-corner pass. X5, who was guarding the ball, rotates on the pass to front the ball-side low post. It's important that X5 sprint to the block and get over any attempt by the ball-side low post player to seal the defender out. X5 then bumps X4 to the ball. X4 must not leave too early, or the low post may be open. X1 rotates to cover the high post and any long pass out of the corner. X3 rotates one step over to cover any attempt to lob to the low post. X3 rebounds the off side, X1 rebounds the middle, X5 rebounds the ball side low post and X4 boxes out the shooter.

If the ball were passed out of the corner to the ball-side wing, these four players would reverse their movements, with X4 bumping X5 out to the ball.

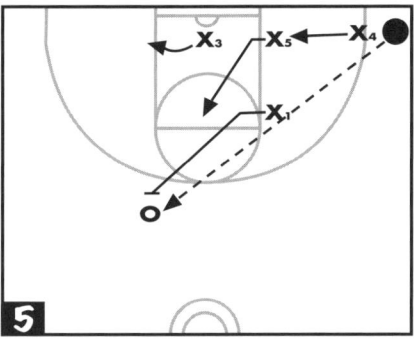

Diagram 5: Player movement on a skip pass out of the corner to a player at the top. X1, seeing a skip pass, immediately moves to close out on the receiver. X5 rotates from the ball-side low post to the middle of the lane, and may go up as high as the free-throw line. This player must be alert for any flashers through the lane. X4 sprints to get between any low post player and the basket. X3 rotates from help side position to fronting the low post.

It's especially important that all four zone defenders be alert to a penetrating drive by the receiver of a skip pass. X1 must close out in such a way as to contain the ball handler.

The Rotating 1-3 and Chaser defense makes an attempt to not only play a zone with man-to-man principles, but also to effectively rotate and cover an opponent's best perimeter shooters.

This defense is not one you could employ for a full game. But it's best utilized when mixed with your main defense, to confuse an opponent and alter strategy for attacking your overall defensive scheme.

FIND MORE BASKETBALL INFORMATION ONLINE

The *Winning Hoops* basketball coaching newsletter staff offers additional valuable coaching information such as news, coaching tips, Web site listings, events and books through a special *FREE* online weekly newsletter called *E-Hoops*. Every issue also includes a valuable motivational quote for your players.

To sign up for this *FREE* weekly e-mail newsletter or if you have valuable coaching information you'd like us to share with other coaches, contact the *Winning Hoops* staff via e-mail at: jsmida@lesspub.com. Our e-mail lists will not be sold to other companies, so you don't have to worry about receiving unwanted e-mails.

*You'll also want to visit the **Winning Hoops** Web site at www.winninghoops.com to receive more coaching tips, tricks and techniques from coaches around the world.*

Chapter 6

Specialties

Many Ingredients For Success In Michigan's Post Double-Team
By Jay Smith

AT THE UNIVERSITY of Michigan we've had a lot of success with the post double-team for a number of reasons. For one thing, it forces your opponent to do something they haven't practiced, and it's difficult to prepare for in a couple of days. It also takes their post player out of the game and changes the post from a scorer to a passer (or forces bad shots or turnovers).

The post double takes your opponent out of their set play and makes them make quick decisions; perimeter jump shots are the usual result.

Another feature of the post double is that it's difficult to scout because the double-teaming comes from different angles.

Finally, the post double keeps your post players out of foul trouble and requires your players to react and communicate — it helps develop the total player.

The basic teaching technique is to double from high opposite the post. When playing the post, you never want the ball to be entered from above the free-throw line extended. The guard should have to dribble down and enter the ball below the free-throw line extended. Also, the post defender should be in a wrap position, denying entry from above and pushing the post player down the lane and holding that player there. As the ball is taken below the free-throw line, a midline is established on which the defense sits. At the same time, we slide behind the post, trying to displace that player off the lane, never allowing him or her to catch the ball directly on the block.

THE DOUBLE

It's very important that your players anticipate from the midline, and at the same time see the ball and assigned player (in case of weak side flashes). Whether a guard or forward is high opposite doesn't matter. We want this player to be quick and aggressive to get a proper angle on the double-team.

On the pass, it's very important not to allow the post player to spin baseline. The post player should be directed toward the middle, forced to turn into the doubler. The doubler shouldn't let the player's shoulders get turned to the point where the post player can spot shooters or cutters on the help side.

The defensive players should press into the post with their chest, and with their arms raised. They should also harass the post and generally create chaos so the post player has problems getting the ball out. Often the post player will become frustrated and try to shoot it out of the double-team, upsetting the coach because the shot is not a high-percentage shot. Note: Good board coverage is needed!

It's also important that the defenders not allow the post to split them. If the offensive player lowers a shoulder, take the charge; it will be called nine times out of ten. Decide as a staff beforehand whether, if the post player reverse pivots and retreats to the sideline with a dribble, to press all the way into that player and keep the double-team on, or to retreat back to your assigned player.

We have had instances where the post player being doubled was a nonscoring big player who hurt us with some passes. A second half adjustment was needed to take the double off and keep it on for everyone else. Teams seem to struggle with that because they work for 3 or 4 days using that player as a decoy and suddenly — "surprise!" — we're not doubling.

OFF-BALL DEFENDERS

It's crucial that the off-ball defenders recognize and react to the post pass coming. Again, they should never lose sight of their own players. We like to drill our players out of the shell concept. We like to add a post player and let that player go block-to-block, working hard to receive the ball in a posting area. Perimeter players may exchange on their side or cut to the basket. Also, in a shell drill, be sure to rotate your players so they get conditioned to all movements and coverages.

Diagram 1: The basic concept of the post double. Defender X5 doesn't let player O5 catch the ball below the free-throw line extended. X5 puts an arm in the passing lane and uses the arm bar to push O5

down the lane, then bumps and slides behind, moving O5 off the lane. Meanwhile, defenders X2 and X4 move into position, anticipating the pass into the post.

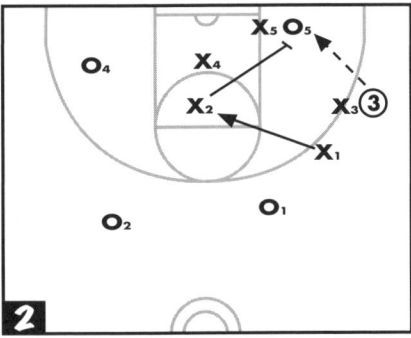

Diagram 2: As O3 passes into the post, defender X2 is there on the catch, pressing into O5. Defender X1 drops into the paint and splits attention between O1 and O2, reading the shoulders, eyes and feet of the post player. X4 can also get a read on the pass, but that player's also the goal tender, reading any cutting action and staying open seeing both ball and assigned player.

If X4 turns and loses sight of O4, you'll be susceptible to easy cuts from the help side. X3 then drops about half a step, never losing sight of ball and opposing player (absolutely never giving up any 3-pointers on the ball side) and not giving O5 an easy pass back out to O3.

On the pass out, the defender must read, react (shoot the gap) and communicate.

Diagram 3: Usually, X1 will take the first pass out and pressure with good closeout, stirring the ball to the outside. X2 will sprint out of

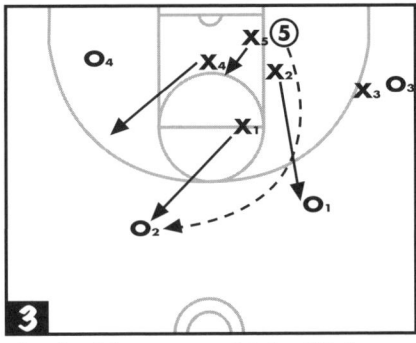

the double-team and take O1 (we don't care about guards and forwards not matching up; our players take the next available player and play half-court defense).

If you don't sprint out of the trap, you'll give up open 3-pointers. The player on the double must quickly read, pass out and move as the ball is in flight. Often X2 (the double) stops, looks and loses one or two crucial seconds of the half-court defense. Remember, on a pass-out, everyone should be shifting, moving and communicating.

Once again, we work this drill out of our four-on-four shell concept by adding a post player and defender. We do this from day one all the way throughout the season, fixing and adjusting different parts as we go along.

SITUATIONS

There have been several situations where we have been forced to alter our concept to accommodate a specific game plan:

1. The Pass Out With Screen In.

Diagram 4: Many times teams have tried and worked on the skip pass out while trying to screen in

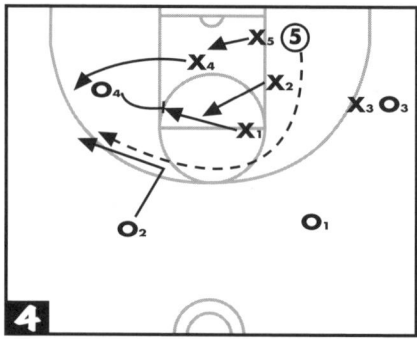

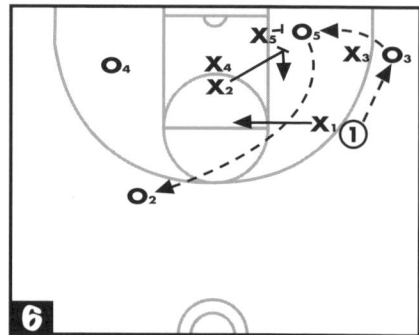

the interceptor. X4 must then be the one who covers out on O2 man. X1 recovers to take player O4, and X2 takes O1. Some might advise O2 to throw it to the O4.

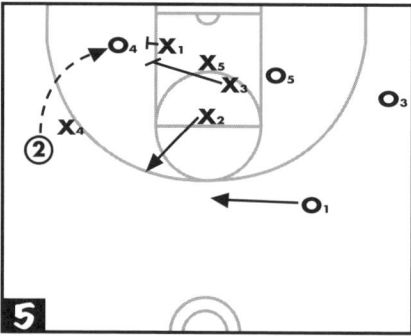

Diagram 5: Now that a guard is on that player (the concept stays consistent), we would be doubling aggressively with defenders X1 and X3.

2. Two Guards Tight On The Ballside.

Diagram 6: The top-side defender X1 has to get into the paint and be the interceptor. For some reason, defenders have a hard time recognizing two players from the same side, below the free-throw line extended. When this happens, it's a different angle on the coverage. Because X1 thinks they're ball side and doesn't get to the coverage

spot, that player should rotate in order to cover both O1 and O2. X1 should get both feet into the paint and try to see the ball and both players, and intercept the pass-out.

3. First Player From The Midline To Get There Is The Doubler.

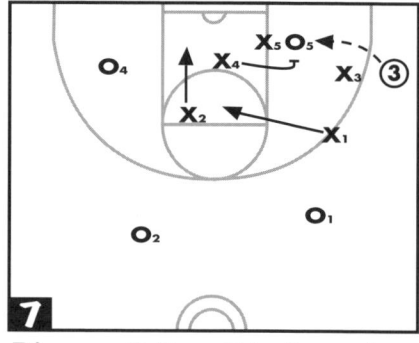

Diagram 7: It could be the goal tender (X4) who doubles, meaning X2 would drop and X1 would still be the interceptor. The rotation would be the same concept discussed earlier. Some players are quicker to read and will be better at doubling than others.

We like to take advantage of this, so we might go to a game of "whoever is the first player from the midline to get there is the doubler." This can be an effective and productive double-team, especially with a veteran team where the players know each other's moves.

4. Covering The Great Shooter On The Help Side If You Leave.

In the past, our team has faced some great shooters, so we've had to make some adjustments, although nothing drastic to our basic philosophy. Several times we've tried putting a different colored jersey on one of our players and made the other players react. We worked on two basic things:
- ✔ Not doubling from the great shooter (this is difficult to do and takes special preparation).
- ✔ Doubling from the great shooter (or cheat toward the shooter, so you give no good looks at the basket).

5. High-Low Concept.

With the size of players nowadays and the way they're able to pass, we see a lot of the high-low concept. When high-low, the post player high will be the doubler or interceptor. Also, we never want the ball entered to the elbow, so we work extremely hard to deny it and try to give an easier look to the low-post player.

6. High Post Player As The Doubler.

Diagram 8: It's usually very difficult to see out of the double-team with two post players. In addition, the post players (defender X4 here) usually love the chance to double.

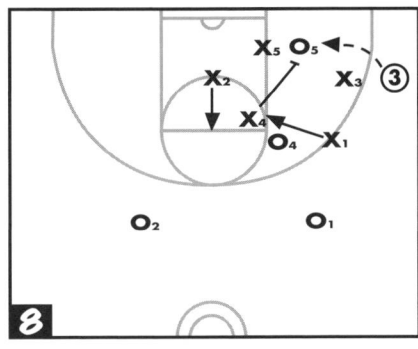

7. Help Side As The Doubler.

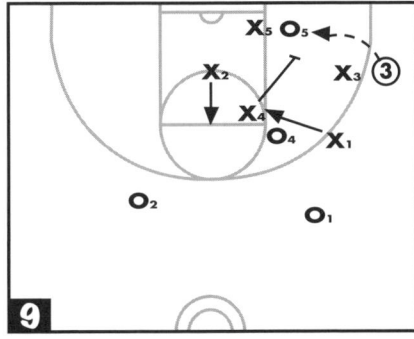

Diagram 9: X2 becomes the double player, X4 rotates to be goal tender and X1 drops into the elbow area to become the interceptor.

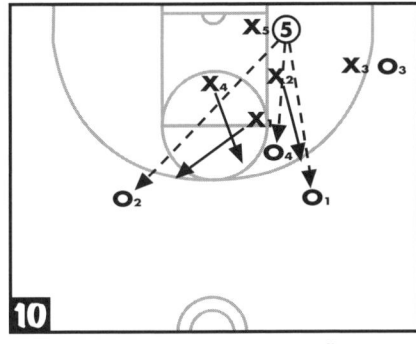

Diagram 10: X1 takes the first pass-out, rotating and communicating.

Defending Four Corners Delay Game
By Pat Sullivan

ONE OF THE most frustrating situations for a coach, is when their team is trailing and the other team begins to go into a four-corners delay game.

Here are a few good ideas for defending a team that is using stalling tactics.

CONCEPTS

The 5-Second Call: Be innovative. By defending the delay game differently, such as by not trapping, your defense will have a chance to create a 5-second call.

Solid One-On-One Defense: If your defense can't force a 5-second call, try to prevent the score with good one-on-one defense.

Go To "Yellow Game": If you fail to defend the delay, you may choose to have your team use a strategy that we call the "Yellow Game." This is based on fouling and attacking offensively to get back into the game.

POINTS OF EMPHASIS

5-Second Call: Try to generate the 5-second call against your opponent by using these concepts:

1. Defenders guarding the ball keep the dribbler in front of them at all times.

2. Other four defenders play total denial.

3. Most delay-game teams are not used to this concept.

4. Force a 5-second call on the dribbler by totally denying the other four offensive players off the ball and keeping the dribbler in front of the assigned defender.

5. If the defender guarding the ball gets beat, instruct your baseline defenders to get in tandem. The high defender in the tandem would try to take the charge or at least stop the ball. The low defender goes toward the pass.

End Of Game Defense When You're Losing
By Pat Sullivan

WHEN YOUR TEAM is trailing and the game is nearing the end, the clock becomes your enemy. You need to figure out a way for your team to stop the clock, regain possession of the ball and score quickly.

Here are some effective tips for playing defense that will help your team catch up, while efficiently saving time on the game clock.

CONCEPTS

Use A Code Name: Have a code name to begin fouling to stop the clock at the end of the game. If you yell to your team to foul, the referees very well may call an intentional foul. We call ours "yellow."

Know Primary Objective: The primary objective is not to foul, but to create the 5-second call or the steal after scoring. Use a fouling strategy only as a last resort.

Court Alignment On Free Throws: After your team fouls to stop the clock, deploy your players on the court so the middle third of the court is open for your point guard to quickly advance the ball.

After the free-throw attempts, you'd like to have your offense create a quality shot in 5 to 10 seconds.

POINTS OF EMPHASIS

26 Press: After we score, we immediately go into our 26 press defense.

✔ On this press, guard the inbounder hard, following the ball with two hands.
✔ Offensive players are guarded in a total denial stance.
✔ Your defenders should hit forearms and switch on all screens so your players can stay in a denial position and hopefully create a 5-second call or get the steal.

INTENTIONALLY FOUL

✔ If your opponent successfully inbounds the ball, foul by aggressively slapping at the ball.
✔ If the referee doesn't see the foul and it causes a turnover, you'll have the ball near your basket for the quick score.
✔ If the referee calls the foul, the clock is stopped and they have to walk all the way to the other end for the free throw. This takes time and helps to ice the shooter.

ON THE FOUL SHOTS
Diagram 1:
✔ If you want a time-out to freeze the free-throw shooter, wait until all lanes are filled and the referee gives the number of shots to be taken. When the referee turns to hand the ball to the shooter, have one of your players step into the lane in front of the official and signal the time-out.
✔ Player deployment for the oppo-

Specialties

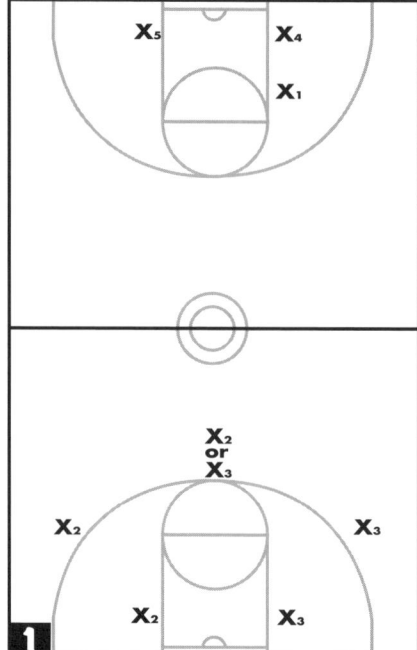

nent's free throw is to fill the first two lanes with X4 and X5. The best shooter of the two should set up on the right side facing the basket. Your point should fill the top lane. X2 and X3 should go to your end of the court.

✔ If X4 is the better shooter between X4 and X5, have X4 inbound the made free throw and trail the play for a possible 3-pointer.

✔ X1 will block out the shooter, then get free for the outlet on the miss or inbound pass on the make.

✔ X2 and X3 will vary their alignments. Have them start on the blocks and cross or they could go baseline and react to 1's penetration from there.

You can also have the X2 and X3 set in tandem at the 3-point line, then spot up on X1's drive.

✔ Make you opponent honor X2 and X3 long, thereby sending two players with them and opening the middle third of the floor for your point guard.

✔ On a missed free throw, have X4 or X5 rebound. After blocking out the shooter, X1 gets the outlet and attacks the basket, looking to create a good shot or look for X2, X3 or X4 as the trailer.

If your team can't get a good shot initially, move into your offensive alignment and look to get the ball to a post player inside.

> "I really believe defense is an art ..."
>
> —Dennis Johnson

Defending Under-The-Basket Inbound Plays
By Pat Sullivan

DEFENDING INBOUND PLAYS under your opponent's basket requires concentration and quality game preparation. An easy inbound pass that results in a quick score for your opponent can be demoralizing for your players.

Emphasize to your players the importance of playing good defense in this situation.

CONCEPTS

5-Second Call: Try to create the 5-second call by taking away all passing lanes for the inbounder.

Make The Steal: If your players don't get the 5-second call, try to steal the inbound pass.

Prevent The Score: If you do not accomplish the above two objectives, try to stop the score.

POINTS OF EMPHASIS

Player Guarding Inbounder: This is a key player to create the 5-second call. Responsibilities are:
✔ Establish position in the middle of the lane in an open stance where the defender can see the inbounder and the other four players on the court.
✔ Be alert in this stance by being a quick head-turner so the inbounder can't bounce the ball off the defender.
✔ Pick up the first cutter to the basket who generally comes off a screen. Follow the first screener quickly to determine who the first cutter to the basket will be.
✔ Stop the first cutter to the basket from getting the ball, then return to the inbounder after the cutter has been picked up by their originally assigned player.

Other Four Players: Have them deny their assigned players the ball. Tell your players not to switch — just aggressively deny their assigned player the ball.
✔ Defenders must guard their assigned player prior to the official placing the ball in play. Many teams like to make quick inbound passes.
✔ The only switch we allow is from a box set when two offensive players at the elbows screen for each other.

Scouting: The key to your execution will come from scouting your opponent's inbound plays.

Walk-Through's: Walk through your inbound play defense. If your defense can create a 5-second call or get the steal, it frustrates your opponent.

Specialties

Changing Defenses Scrambles An Offense
By Bill Graf

YOUR DEFENSE SHOULD be your best offense. By constantly changing defenses, your team will create confusion, cause disruptions to the offensive flow and generally control the tempo of the game.

This style of play is very versatile. We have used this attack when we've had talented teams and when our talent was sparse. We never approached this as something we would do with a less talented team just so we could stay in ball games.

CHANGE SEQUENCE

When our players walk into the locker room before a game there are seven numbers on the board. These will be our starting defenses. We're going to play seven defenses depending on what we do on offense or where the opponent is taking the ball out of bounds. The sequence of defenses is as follows:

1. Made field goals.
2. Missed field goals.
3. Made free throws.
4. Missed free throws.
5. Sideline out-of-bounds (back court).
6. Sideline out-of-bounds (front court).
7. Baseline out-of-bounds.

Play full-court pressure defense on made goals, free throws and side out in the backcourt because those situations afford your team time to set up. Against teams who like to walk the ball up court, you can also use full-court pressure on misses.

On missed field goals and free throws, play a half-court defense and use half-court traps against teams who don't play an up-tempo offense.

DIFFERENT LOOKS

The possibility of multiple combinations on defense is unlimited. Our teams used eight full-court defenses, five different half-court traps, several gimmick or "junk" defenses, several straight or conventional half-court zones and a basic man-to-man. The following are just a few of the different defensive looks we can give an opposing team:

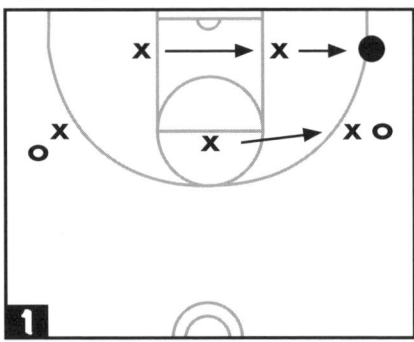

Diagram 1: Triangle And 2. The top defender covers elbow to elbow. When the ball is on the baseline, the bottom defender slides out and the other low defender crosses the lane and fronts any post player.

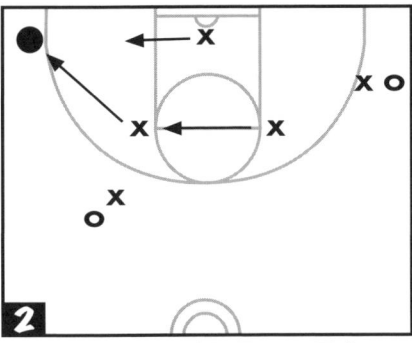

Diagram 2: Upside Down Triangle And 2. When the ball is on the baseline, the defender on the ball-side elbow slides down to cover. Bottom defender fronts and off-side defender goes to other elbow.

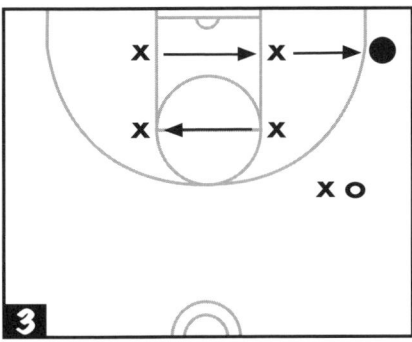

Diagram 3: Box And 1. When the ball is on the baseline, the bottom defender slides out to cover, the off-side bottom defender crosses and fronts, and the off-side elbow defender drops to become back-side rebounder.

Diagram 4: "Freak." The defense changes when the ball is dribbled or passed on the perimeter to swing the side. If it's a skip pass over the top crossing the center line, stay in your initial defense.

Diagram 5: "State." Top defender covers elbows. Bottom defenders use conventional 2-3 zone slides.

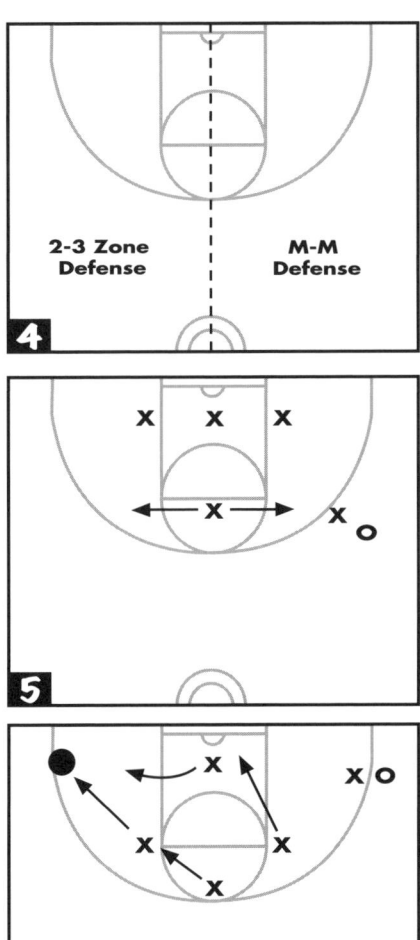

Diagram 6: Diamond And 1. When the ball is on the baseline, the wing defender on that side slides down to cover, the top defender goes to elbow area, bottom defender fronts and the off-side wing defender becomes the back-side rebounder.

Diagram 7: Rover. This starts out looking like a conventional 2-3 zone until the ball is passed to an

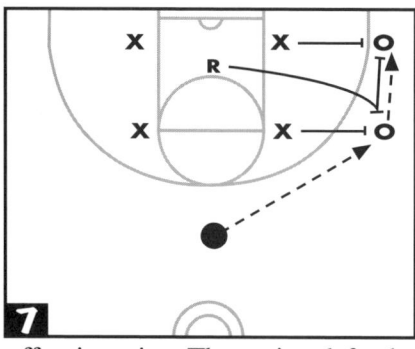

offensive wing. The roving defender doubles the ball wherever it is on the floor.

OTHER SUGGESTIONS

Double team out of regular and half-court zones or man defense on a designated pass. For example, wherever your third pass occurs, start your continuous double teaming.

In other situations depending on your scouting reports, designate your traps to start on a pass to a wing or a dribble to a wing. We like to double team on offensive screens because it brings two offensive players together and makes them susceptible to turnovers.

Your players have to discipline themselves to learn all the defenses and sequences. If they can't master the mental aspect of the game, their playing time and team effectiveness will be affected. Our coaching staff feels that mental mistakes are worse than physical ones.

THE RIGHT TIMING

So when do you change defenses? Change at time-outs, half way through quarters, between quarters, half time, during the lining up for a free throw and in transition.

As the players are running down the floor into defensive transition, yell out the new defense. You may change the whole sequence (seven defenses) or just field goal or free-throw defenses.

We've been very disruptive playing a box and 1 or a triangle and 2 vs. baseline plays. Part of the reasoning is to keep the ball away from your opponent's main offensive threats. We've also gone into continuous double teams on the first pass in bounds off a man or zone baseline defense. Always change baseline defenses at the start of each quarter.

BUILDING BLOCKS

All three teams in our high school program used changing defenses. Start your freshmen off with the made/missed field goal or free-throw sequences. They'll catch on to the system and have fun having success with it.

After a year, your junior varsity players should be able to run the entire sequence. We've played as many as two dozen defenses in one game.

We've even had situations with this system where a player makes a mistake (a wrong alignment or incorrect slide) and still gets a steal. This is due to the confusion the changing defenses have caused. When teams come down the floor and have to think about what defense they're facing, it hampers offensive efficiency.

The foundation for all our defensive sets is a sound understanding and teaching of man-to-man defense. I've observed in many NCAA tournaments that teams who change up on defense did very well.

Over the years, we've had coaches tell our staff how difficult it is to prepare to play us. This compliment reinforces our confidence in the "changing defenses" philosophy.

Using Multiple Defenses Gives Your Team A Winning Edge
By Thom Sigel

ALL COACHES IN team sports have probably used the old slogan "Defense Wins Championships" at one time or another. Basketball coaches throughout the country at all levels can attest to the truth in that slogan. The top teams in your league have likely invested planning, time and practice in developing a top-notch defense.

When the other teams on your schedule are dedicated to playing good defense, you must also dedicate yourself to winning with defense. Buying into the philosophy of using multiple defenses can give your team the edge it needs to win the big games.

Some coaches hold with the philosophy that man-to-man defense is the only defense to play, especially in this era of the 3-point shot. There is no doubt in my mind that the principles of man-to-man defense comprise the basis for all defenses. Coaches who use a zone, zone presses or match-up zones teach these defenses using drills that emphasize the principles of man-to-man. Thus, the argument of not having the time to spend teaching the different defenses is not valid, since they all can be developed from the regular defensive drills most coaches already use.

We consistently teach defense by using drills to instruct guarding the ball, the passing lanes and post players. It's also essential to use the four and six player shell drills on a regular basis. I believe that from these and other universal defensive drills, it's not difficult for a coach to teach, or a player to learn, many half-court and full-court defenses.

The fact that many defenses can be developed from basic man-to-man principles does not by itself explain why there's an advantage to using multiple defenses.

There are four specific ways using multiple defenses can help

your team win. Using multiple defenses:
1. Allows flexibility for certain opponents and situations.
2. Is important in game preparation.
3. Confuses the opponent's point guard.
4. Can win a game where a single possession is critical to the outcome. Let's look at these advantages more closely.

FLEXIBILITY

In addition to giving your team great versatility, using multiple defenses also allows you to have many options against a variety of opponents or for the different situations that can develop in games. Coaches face many different types of teams; quick, slow, big, small, outside-oriented, inside-oriented, teams that run set plays or teams that run a good motion offense. Because of the various offensive styles you'll encounter, it's an advantage to have a variety of defenses from which to choose when trying to defend them. Using one defense exclusively will win you the games against teams for which your defense happens to be best suited. But teams with different strengths may be able to take advantage of that same defense. I believe in trying to win every game with any defense that may be necessary.

There are also situations that warrant the use of multiple defenses, such as being in foul trouble, facing mismatches or playing from behind. When your best defensive player gets in foul trouble in a tight game, having another defense to go to is a blessing. Trying to give a mini-lesson on a new defense during a time-out or taking this player out, even for a minute, can cost your team the game.

Having a variety of defenses also allow you to negate a great offensive player by giving extra help or hiding your poorest defensive player. You can also double a great offensive player threat. In addition, playing from behind can be an uphill battle when you have only one defense, which actually may have helped put you in the hole in the first place. When an opposing team comes out well prepared and has success offensively, the answer may be to go to another defensive plan that your team already knows.

GAME PREPARATION

Using multiple defenses makes your game preparation more complete by saving time and helping to confuse your opponents. It allows you to practice those that will best defend an upcoming opponent. Including in your game plan two or three defenses that would be successful against an upcoming opponent can make your preparation easier.

The versatility of using multiple defenses allows you to focus on refining certain aspects of defenses you've already practiced rather than focusing on the strengths of your opponent. Taking the time to restructure your only defense to stop a very good offensive team is difficult and time-consuming. This is especially important in post-season play, where typically there may be only one or two days to prepare.

Another factor in game preparation involves your opponents. They may scout you in a game where you play one defense, while you plan on using a different defense against them. Also, if you play numerous defenses well in a game they scout, they'll have to spend practice time preparing to go against all of them. Having to prepare for several defenses would cut the time they'd have to focus on other aspects of their offense they might need to do well to beat you.

CONFUSING THE POINT GUARD

Being a former point guard, I can tell you that the most disrupting thing opponents did to us was change defenses during a game. If you can get the opposing guard to begin guessing, you've taken the first step toward disrupting their offense. Even if you have a good press as your only defense, a team with a good guard can beat it if the player has been prepared and knows it's coming every possession.

By using a variety of half-court man-to-man and zone defenses as well as at least one press during the week, you can take the opposing team out of their game plan by mixing up your defenses and confusing their point guard. The opposing coach may need to burn a time-out or two to discuss adjustments.

ONE-POSSESSION GAME

Many games are decided on one possession. If your team is able to make a defensive change late in a tight game, it has a great chance of confusing the offense, forcing them to take bad shots or commit turnovers.

Another situation in a close game where having a number of defenses to use can turn the tide in your favor is after a time-out. For instance, if the opposing coach calls time-out to set up a play, you could gum up the works by switching defenses. Even if a possession does not have the outcome of the game riding on it, it may help win the game by shifting the momentum to your team.

Some of the defenses we used when I was coaching at Galesburg High School in Illinois were straight man-to-man, three trapping man-to-man defenses, three levels of zone presses and a match-up zone. By using these defenses against different opponents and mixing them up during games, we had achieved a measure of success in recent years, and our program had gotten a reputation for being tough on defense.

I believe you must have one defense that is your bread-and-butter defense and that the entire team has confidence to go to during crunch time. When you've developed one defense you can call your own, use basic defensive principles and drills to practice other defenses. If you can use multiple defenses effectively during games and preparation time, they'll help you win a lot of games.

Defending The 3-Point Shot
By Roger Lyons

THE 3-POINT SHOT has changed the game of basketball. It has been the single most important rule change since the elimination of the jump ball after every score and the widening of the free-throw lane. Coaches are now becoming comfortable incorporating the 3-point shot into their regular offensive scheme. It's no longer simply a tool used to catch up or a big play momentum changer.

The attitude toward the 3-point shot is also changing defensively. We can no longer ignore the team or player who shoots from "3" consistently. Defensive techniques must be taught that cover the offense and take away the good look from the 3-point line.

In defending the 3-point shot, we teach defensive techniques in four basic areas:
1. Defensive conversion.
2. Ball-side coverage.
3. Help-side coverage.
4. Player identification.

DEFENSIVE CONVERSION

Coaches preach the importance of getting back on defense and building from the basket out. With many offensive teams releasing their 3-point threats early and down the floor to open spots, conversion to the perimeter is now vital. The old concept (basket out) gives way to the new concept of converting to 3-point shooter on the perimeter and expecting teammates to run help side and cover the basket area.

We insist on the following in our defensive fast break conversion:

✔ **After Opponent's Defensive Rebound.** We attack the first pass made (usually to a guard). We try to slow the ball, control the break and stop ball penetration.

✔ **Sprint Defensive Lanes.** Lane recognition becomes as important on defense as it is on offense. We do not want two defensive players in conversion guarding one lane.

✔ **Half-Turn At Half-Court.** We need to "see the ball" as quickly as possible and determine ball side from help side. A full turn requires backpedaling, which is usually too slow. The half-turn is quicker and allows the defensive player to continue to run.

✔ **Locate, Cover, Zone Up.** We locate any player who appears in our defensive conversion lane, cover out quickly to identified 3-point threat and zone up on basket coverage behind the player or players who converted to the perimeter. The first pass across half-court is dangerous for the defense and usually results in an open 3-point look for the offensive fast-break team. This pass must be covered quickly.

✔ **Communication.** We're more interested in lane coverage vs. the fast break than in seeking a particular defensive match-up. We'll readjust to assigned match-ups only upon shutting down the offensive break or in a dead-ball situation. Great defensive talk must occur in recognizing lane responsibility, location of 3-point shooting threats and any changes in coverage.

Without communication among players, our defensive fast break conversion will break down and allow the two things we're working hard to cover — an open look from the 3-point line and easy baskets off the break.

When our defensive fast break conversion is successful and we force the offense to attack our man-to-man defense in a half-court set, the techniques for defending the 3-point shooter are organized into ball side and help side coverages.

BALL SIDE COVERAGE

The following points apply to our ball-side coverage scheme:

✔ **One-On-One Individual Defense-Controlling Dribble Penetration.** It's important that players recognize the simple concept of keeping the ball as far away from the basket as possible. Anytime the ball can be penetrated on the dribble, the defense usually reacts to help in the driving lane. This allows the penetrator to draw two defenders and pitch to an open player for a 3-pointer.

The ability to control the ball on the perimeter and stay away from ball-side help to recover situations allows for very few uncontested 3-point opportunities.

✔ **Staying Home.** Within our defensive scheme, we will ask all five defenders not to leave a designated player open at the 3-point line for any chance to receive the ball. This calls for defenders to be disciplined, to concentrate and to identify. It also requires them to not react on ball side penetration. This nonreaction is against normal defensive instinct and can be very difficult to execute.

✔ **Use Of The Aggressive Switch.** In covering the 3-point shot, we ask our defense to switch out and jump-switch. The switch out usually occurs vs. the wing-to-block downscreen. We ask our players to switch early and into the 3-point shot passing lane. The mismatch with a big player posting a small player must be handled by great ball pressure when the offensive perimeter player receives the ball. With this switch we also encourage the ball to go into the 2-point scoring area.

The jump-switch occurs when

Specialties

the 3-point shooter comes behind the ball handler (in a weave) or replaces on ball penetration. This is a very difficult 3-point shot to defend, but it can be done if the defensive players see the situation early, aggressively jump to switch and talk to guarantee coverage.

✔ **Force The Ball-Side Backcut.** In special situations, we'll take away all 3-point shot attempts at the expense of giving up a good 2-point shot. This usually occurs at the end of a quarter or half, or at the end of a game, when the offense needs a 3-point basket to change momentum or to tie or win a game. The defense is asked to get closer to the potential 3-point receiver and allow the ball to be caught only inside the 3-point line. This gives the offensive player only one option on the ball side, and that is to backcut.

HELP-SIDE COVERAGE

The following points are applicable to our help-side coverage scheme:

✔ **Positioning.** The ability to rotate from the help side to stop the ball and support a teammate is the essence of team defense. Without the complete trust that teammates will fill to the ball and provide help, ball pressure and sound ball-side coverage usually break down. Yet, with the 3-point shot becoming a potent offensive weapon, help side positioning has changed.

No longer can the help side defender afford the luxury of "splitting the lane on the help line," with the main point of attention on rotation to the ball and stopping penetration. Coaches must now insist on and teach better one-on-one individual defense to allow the help side defender more of an opportunity to shade toward the weak-side 3-point shooting threat.

Offensive coaches teach and encourage the skip pass or quick ball reversal to get a 3-pointer. Both of these situations make it important for the help side defender to be in a position to become a ball side defender at the 3-point line quickly. If the help-side defender is buried deep in the lane, the chance to cover out at 3-point range is reduced.

As a rule, we ask our help-side defenders to have one foot in the key area. Rotation to ball penetration must be quick and at full speed, coverage of the 3-point line done with accurate closeouts.

✔ **Closeouts.** The term closeout is relatively new in defensive teaching. It stresses the concept of going from being a help-side defender to a quick ball-side defender and being able to close up on the ball to control or cover the offensive threat.

We organize our closeouts into two types — closeout long and closeout short.

Closeout Long: Is designed to cover the 3-point shooter and distract the long-shot attempt. We ask the defensive player to:

A. Run (not slide) toward the offensive player (quickness to the shooter!).

B. Attack with hands up.
C. Fly at the shooting hand, trying to force a change in shot rhythm.
D. Force the 3-point shooter to become a driver and take the ball inside the 2-point scoring area.
E. Quickly recover back into the play in case of a long rebound in the direction of the shooter.

Closeout Short: Is designed to encourage the 3-point shot and contain the ball on dribble penetration. We ask the defensive player to:

A. Run to within 6 feet of the shooter and then "break down" (change body momentum, take small chop steps, force weight back).
B. Keep hands up, in a position that will not distract but will help defensive slide movement.
C. Stop the initial dribble penetration and encourage the offensive player to become a 3-point shooter.
D. Close up on the killed dribble and take away any free look to the post or to a cutter. This can be done only with great ball pressure.
E. Check the shooter and take away any free lane to the offensive board.

PLAYER IDENTIFICATION

In defending the 3-point shot, it's crucial to determine who on the opposing team can shoot it and who can't. This can be done through the use of statistics, scouting reports and tape evaluation.

As a defensive game plan is formulated, the coaching staff must be able to determine what tendencies the 3-point shooters have from that range. For example, do they like to shoot off the dribble or off the pass? Are they better going left or going right? Where in the 3-point area are they usually positioned.

Armed with information on the opposing team, we can decide who must be closed out long and who must be closed out short. Each defensive player must recognize who they have in their area and which closeout technique to use.

During a game, the coaching staff will be able to make adjustments and defend areas that are hurting the defense. One way this can be done is by changing the closeout scheme for a particular player. If an opponent is cold but continues to shoot from "3," we'll defend that player with short closeouts only. Long closeouts are used to cover the player with the hot hand.

The 3-point shot has brought excitement and the age of the specialist to basketball offense. As the "trifecta" continues to grow in popularity, coaches will continue to work hard to develop techniques to "cover at 3." As the offense goes, the defense is never that far behind.

Find Rock-Solid Answers To Your Most Pressing Coaching Problems With These Winning Hoops Special Coaching Reports

Geared to helping you find game-tested, highly practical solutions to specific basketball coaching concerns.

Out-Of-Bounds Strategies

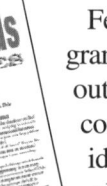

Featuring exciting plays and easy-to-follow diagrams, you'll get the latest thinking on game-winning, out-of-bounds strategies from highly successful coaches. This Special Coaching Report offers fresh ideas to help you create more scoring opportunities, shows you how to develop a versatile underneath attack, outlines key strategies and offers valuable game-winning plays for critical situations.

(8 pages) **$6.95**

Scouting The Opposition

An in-depth look at the techniques involved in preparing a complete scouting report on your opponents is found in this Special Coaching Report. Learn how to decide what scouting data is most important, how to effectively handle scouting duties and how to capitalize on the valuable information your assistants bring back.

There's a comparison of various scouting methods, explanations of how to fully utilize scouting information in your practices and suggestions on effectively using video scouting to develop your own customized scouting report!

(8 pages) **$6.95**

Buzzer Beaters

Does your team lack that killer instinct? Are you losing too many games in the final seconds?

Get back on track with this Special Coaching Report that's jam-packed with the very best ideas on how to prepare for end-of-game situations, special plays to use in the closing seconds and how to keep your players poised and confident during crunch time.

(8 pages) **$6.95**

Off-Season/In-Season Individual Workouts

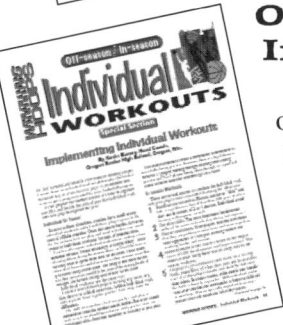

While every coach knows it's valuable to work as a team on the court, it's also important to fully develop the skill levels of your individual players. This Special Coaching Report will help you do just that, since it's packed with valuable information on helping you find new ways to help your players strengthen individual abilities.

(8 pages) **$6.95**

Building Better Assistants

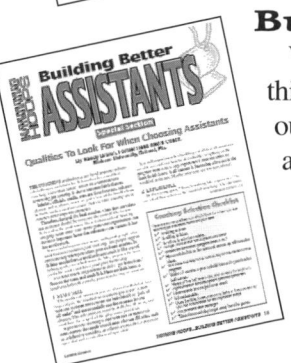

While it's not easy to find the perfect assistant coach, this Special Coaching Report authored by a half-dozen outstanding high school and college coaches offers valuable ideas to get the recruiting and interviewing job done.

Regardless of the level at which you coach, this Special Coaching Report offers time-tested ideas to help you find the right person for added bench strength. It's also loaded with valuable tips to help you climb the ladder to that ultimate coaching position.

(8 pages) **$6.95**

Order These Valuable Reports Today!

Each 8-page *Winning Hoops* Special Coaching Report is only $6.95 with **FREE** shipping and handling for U.S. and Canadian orders.

Please add $2.50 for foreign shipments for each report.
Payable in U.S. funds drawn on a U.S. bank only.
Wisconsin resident need to add 5.1 percent sales tax.

See page 159 for ordering instructions.

Priority Code: CHPDEF

Save 58%
On 3 Great Reports!

BASKETBALL DRILLS
Includes 67 drills — shooting drills, defensive drills, conditioning drills and multipurpose drills. This 24-page book features the best drills used by successful high school and college coaches. Normally $19.95 — yours for just
$9.95, with FREE shipping and handling!

BASKETBALL DEFENSE
Top coaches provide different defensive formations and valuable insights on how to outthink your opponents. Learn from plenty of coaching tips jammed into this 24-page book on how to beat screens, overcome picks, block out under the boards, establish proper defensive positioning and instill the necessary attitude your players need to shutdown foes. Normally $19.95 — yours for just
$9.95, with FREE shipping and handling!

BASKETBALL PLAYS
Top college and high school coaches share last-second plays that have snatched victory from the jaws of defeat, plays to get you that all-important offensive rebound off a missed free throw and that last-second inbounds play to defeat a man-to-man defense. This 24-page book outlines 16 options out of a box set and unique plays for successful three-point shots. Some 78 plays cover every possible game situation. Normally $19.95 — yours for just
$9.95, with FREE shipping and handling!

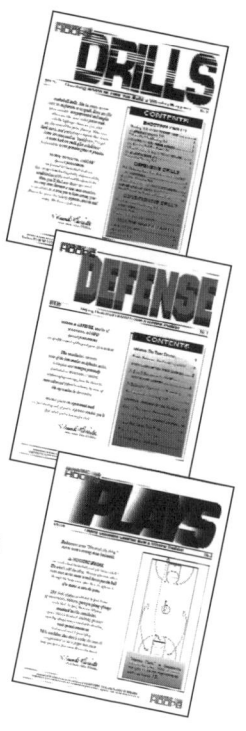

• •
Get Defense, Drills and Plays!
72 combined pages...only $24.95* with FREE shipping and handling!

Buy these three reports as a set for only $24.95 and save 58% off the regular price. A $59.85! value! You'll get the top drills, defense and scoring plays proven by the best coaches in the country. Get these three reports and start improving your team's record today!

To Order Mail To:
Winning Hoops, P.O. Box 624, Brookfield, WI 53008-0624
For Faster Service In The U.S., Call: **(800) 645-8455** Or **(262) 782-4480**
Or Fax To: **(262) 782-1250** • E-mail: **info@lesspub.com**
Web site: **www.winninghoops.com**

*Payable in U.S. Funds drawn on a U.S. bank only. Wis. residents add 5.1% sales tax. Shipping and handling is free in the U.S. and Canada! Foreign orders add $2.50 per set.

Priority Code: CHPDEF

NEED FRESH BLACKBOARD PLAYS?

When you're stumped for a play to run in certain situations, wouldn't it be nice to pick up a book with an abundance of game-tested plays?

You can do just that with the more than 200 plays collected from coaches at the top of their game found in the 128 pages of *Blackboard Strategies*. Neatly organized and instantly accessible with plenty of diagrams, you'll find plenty of solutions to these coaching concerns:

- ✔ Side Out-Of-Bounds.
- ✔ Baseline Out-Of-Bounds.
- ✔ Quick Hitters.
- ✔ Plays Vs. Zones.
- ✔ Plays Vs. Man-To-Man.
- ✔ Plays To Start Specific Offenses.
- ✔ Last-Second Plays.
- ✔ Gimmick Plays.

Submitted by winning coaches, these are the most exciting blackboard plays to have appeared in 15 years of *Winning Hoops*.

Each 128-page book is $14.95.

Please add $4 for shipping and handling for the first book and $1 shipping and handling for each additional book.

Wisconsin residents need to add 5.1 percent sales tax.

For foreign and Canadian orders, add $8 to the cover price for the first book and $5 to the cover price for each additional book.

Payable in U.S. funds drawn on a U.S. bank only.

See page 159 for ordering instructions.

Priority Code: CHPDEF

Add More Power To Your Team's Play!

Coming from the playbooks of more than 40 of the most successful coaches in the game, these 55 outstanding drills will improve your ballplayers' skill levels in key areas:

- Ball handling.
- Shooting.
- Defense and Rebounding.
- Conditioning and Stretching.
- Offense.
- All-Around Complete Game.

Covering all aspects of the game, these drills have been run by some of the game's best coaches and are sure to work for you. Use the innovative drills found in this 100-page book that's jammed with plenty of diagrams to take your team's play to the next level.

Each 100-page book is $13.95.

Please add $4 for shipping and handling for the first book and $1 shipping and handling for each additional book.
Wisconsin residents need to add 5.1 percent sales tax.
For foreign and Canadian orders, add $8 to the cover price for the first book and $5 to the cover price for each additional book.
Payable in U.S. funds drawn on a U.S. bank only.
See page 159 for ordering instructions.

Priority Code: CHPDEF

Winning Basketball Offense...

From 40 Of America's Winningest Coaches!

The most effective execution of man-to-man, zone, motion, fast-break, flex, shuffle, triangle and press offenses are featured in 200 diagrams and text in this 100-page book from the *Winning Hoops* editors.

In addition, a special situations chapter shows you how to cash in on three-point shots, inbounds plays, isolation plays and weak-side action plays.

When it comes to offensive game strategies, nobody diagrams X's and O's better than these 40 coaches. These 40 outstanding contributors have over 400 years of combined basketball coaching experience, including 20 coaches each with over two decades of coaching success.

Each 100-page book is $12.95.
PLUS $4 FOR SHIPPING AND HANDLING FOR THE 1ST BOOK
AND $1 SHIPPING AND HANDLING FOR EACH ADDITIONAL BOOK.
WISCONSIN RESIDENTS ADD 5.1% SALES TAX.

To Order, Mail To:
Winning Hoops • P.O. Box 624 • Brookfield, WI 53008-0624
For Faster Service In The U.S., Call: (800) 645-8455 Or (262) 782-4480
Or Fax To: (262) 782-1252 • E-mail: info@lesspub.com
Web site: www.winninghoops.com
with credit card information.

Payable in U.S. Funds drawn on a U.S. bank only.
For foreign and Canadian orders, add $8 to the cover price for shipping and handling for the first book and $5 to the cover price for each additional book.
Special Coaching Reports ship FREE for U.S. and Canadian orders.
Please add $2.50 for foreign shipments for each report.

Priority Code: CHPDEF

WINNING HOOPS...
LIKE HAVING ANOTHER ASSISTANT COACH ON YOUR BENCH!

If you want to win more games, subscribe to this award-winning practical "X's and O's" publication which is jammed with plays, diagrams and techniques for basketball coaches at all levels—from well-known NBA and Division 1 college coaches to men and women coaching grade school kids as volunteers.

This six-times-a-year newsletter features solid coaching skills, plays, diagrams, techniques, drills and hoops management ideas that you can put to immediate use. Must reading for basketball coaches at every level.

SEND WINNING HOOPS TO FRIENDS!

This six-times-a-year newsletter also makes a great gift for friends coaching basketball at any level of competition. This newsletter makes a great gift that takes on all aspects of basketball coaching:

- ✔ Defense.
- ✔ Drills.
- ✔ Free throws.
- ✔ Game preparation.
- ✔ Game management.
- ✔ Offense.
- ✔ Personal coaching growth.
- ✔ Coaching philosophies.
- ✔ Player and family relations.
- ✔ Player motivation.
- ✔ Practice management.
- ✔ Hi-tech computer ideas for coaches.
- ✔ Promotion and marketing of a basketball program.

It's a great learning tool that will help you win more games — practically like having another assistant coach sitting on your bench all year long!

For subscription information, contact:
Winning Hoops • P.O. Box 624 • Brookfield, WI 53008-0624
For Faster Service In The U.S., Call: **(800) 645-8455** Or **(262) 782-4480**
Or Fax To: **(262) 782-1252** • E-mail: **info@lesspub.com**
Web site: **www.winninghoops.com**

Priority Code: CHPDEF